CLEANSING RURAL DUBLIN

T0167964

Maynooth Studies in Irish Local History

SERIES EDITOR   Raymond Gillespie

This is one of six new pamphlets in the Maynooth Studies in Irish Local History Series to be published in the year 2001 which brings the number published to forty. Like their predecessors most of the pamphlets are based on theses completed as part of the M.A. in local history programme in National University of Ireland, Maynooth. While the regions and time span which they cover are diverse, from Cork city to Tyrone, they all share a conviction that the exploration of the local past can shed light on the evolution of modern societies. They each demonstrate that understanding the evolution of local societies is important. The local worlds of Ireland in the past are as complex and sophisticated as the national framework in which they are set. The communities which peopled those local worlds, whether they be the inhabitants of large cities, housing on the edge of those cities or rural estates, shaped and were shaped by their environments to create a series of inter-locking worlds of considerable complexity. Those past worlds are best interpreted not through local administrative divisions, such as the county, but in human units: local places where communities of people lived and died. Untangling what held these communities together, and what drove them apart, gives us new insights into the world we have lost.

These pamphlets each make a significant contribution to understanding Irish society in the past. Together with thirty-four earlier works in this series they explore something of the hopes and fears of those who lived in Irish local communities in the past. In doing so they provide examples of the practice of local history at its best and show the vibrant discipline which the study of local history in Ireland has become in recent years.

Maynooth Studies in Irish Local History: Number 40

Cleansing rural Dublin: public health and housing initiatives in the South Dublin Poor Law Union 1880–1920

Frank Cullen

IRISH ACADEMIC PRESS

DUBLIN • PORTLAND, OR

First published in 2001 by
IRISH ACADEMIC PRESS
44, Northumberland Road, Dublin 4, Ireland
and in the United States of America by
IRISH ACADEMIC PRESS
c/o ISBS, 5824 NE Hassalo Street, Portland, OR 97213–3644.

website: www.iap.ie

© Frank Cullen 2001

British Library Cataloguing in Publication Data
Cullen, Frank
    Cleansing rural Dublin: public health and housing initiatives in the South Dublin
    Poor Law Union, 1880–1920. – (Maynooth research guides for Irish local history;
    no. 40)
    1. Public health – Ireland – Dublin – History – 19th century   2. Public health –
    Ireland – Dublin – History – 20th century   3. Public housing – Ireland –
    Dublin – History – 19th century   4. Public housing – Ireland – Dublin –
    History – 20th century   5. Dublin (Ireland) – Social conditions – 19th century
    6. Dublin (Ireland) – Social conditions – 20th century   7. Ireland – Politics and
    government – 1837–1901   8. Ireland – Politics and government – 1901–1910
    9. Ireland – Politics and government – 1910–1921
    I. Title
    362'.094183'09034
    ISBN 0–7165–2738–3

A catalog record of this book is available from the Library of Congress

Typeset in 10 pt on 12 pt Bembo by
Carrigboy Typesetting Services, County Cork
Printed by Creative Print and Design (Wales) Ebbw Vale

Contents

Acknowledgements   vii

Introduction   I

1   Geographical perspectives: the South Dublin Poor Law Union   4

2   Environmental management: public health challenges   12

3   Rural housing reform: addressing the plight of the
agricultural labourer   35

Conclusion   53

Notes   57

FIGURES

1   Dublin Poor Law Unions. Based on the general map of Ireland
showing poor law union and electoral division boundaries (1891)   5

2   South Dublin Poor Law Union and Electoral Divisions.
Based on the general map of Ireland showing poor law
union and electoral division boundaries (1891)   8

3   Clondalkin village, c.1840, watercolour, artist unknown   10

4   Sir Charles Alexander Cameron, chief medical officer
of health for Dublin, 1880–1912   13

5   Loretto House, Rathfarnham, Dublin, c.1850, by G. Du Noyer   16

6   River Dodder at Lord Ely's Gate, Rathfarnham, Dublin, artist
unknown   18

7   Tallaght, County Dublin, extract from Ordnance Survey 1:10,560,
sheets 21, 22 revision of 1871, 1869. Permit No MP001501   23

8   Terenure, Dublin, extract from Ordnance Survey 1:10,560,
sheet 22, revision of 1869. Permit No MP001501   24

9   Rathfarnham, County Dublin, showing St Patrick's Cottages,
    extract from Ordnance Survey 1:10,560, sheet 22, revision
    of 1869. Permit No MP001501   31

10 Cabin near Finglass, attributed to Brocas family   37

11 Clondalkin, County Dublin, showing St Bridget's Cottages,
    extract from Ordnance Survey 1:10,560, sheets 17, 21,
    revision of 1870, 1871. Permit No MP001501   42

12 St Bridget's Cottages, Bushelloaf, Clondalkin, built 1902
    (Photograph by F. Cullen)   45

13 No. 1 St Patrick's Cottages, Rathfarnham, built 1901
    (Photograph by F. Cullen)   47

TABLES

1   Area, valuation and population of Dublin Poor Law Unions
    in 1881   7

2   Lands and cottages proposed to be taken compulsorily,
    by way of absolute purchase, and names of owners, lessees
    and occupiers interested therein   40

3   Provisional order for purchasing lands to build cottages
    (under the Labourers' (Ireland) Acts) showing townlands
    where land is situated   41

Acknowledgements

I would like to acknowledge the support and advice of a number of people and institutions during the course of this study. My initial thanks must go to my MA supervisor, Dr Jacinta Prunty whose stimulating ideas and endless encouragement were invaluable throughout. I am also indebted to Professor R.V. Comerford, Head of Department, and Dr Raymond Gillespie for their kind help and support during my period of study at Maynooth. Sincere thanks also go to the following persons and institutions for making the material available to me: Ms Tina Hynes, Fingal County Council Archive, the National Library of Ireland, the National Archives, the Library of the Royal College of Physicians of Ireland, the Library of the Royal College of Surgeons in Ireland, the Royal Irish Academy and the John Paul II Library, Maynooth.

I would also like to thank the Ordnance Survey of Ireland for permission to reproduce maps, and the Prints and Drawings Department of the National Library of Ireland for permission to reproduce prints. The maps shown in Figures 1 and 2 are my own drawings based on the general map of Ireland showing poor law union and electoral division boundaries (1891), reproduced from the Map Library, Trinity College Library Dublin, with the permission of the Board of Trinity College.

My family has shown great interest in this work from the very beginning, to them I am most grateful, particularly to my fiancée, Paula, who has shown me continued support throughout. Finally, I would like to dedicate this book to my parents, Frank and Peg, in acknowledgement of their unwavering support and endless encouragement throughout my life.

Introduction

This pamphlet addresses the important issue of public health in the late nineteenth century, using the territorial boundaries of the South Dublin Poor Law Union as its geographical unit of study. As a study in local history it is concerned primarily with the lives of the local inhabitants of this area, and more specifically, with the impact on these lives of local government politics. Its primary objective therefore, is to explore from both an administrative and social perspective, the trials and tribulations involved in implementing within this union, the Public Health (Ireland) Act, 1878. Throughout the work, emphasis is placed on two related themes. First, the state's reaction to the appalling conditions of public health then prevalent within this and many other rural areas is examined, especially through the implementation of the above legislation. The second theme examines the impact of this legislation on the lives of the local inhabitants, particularly the agricultural labourers and their families, and examines their collective response to the social change brought about by these government measures.

For the local historian, Dublin has been the subject of a vast amount of study, both city-wide and parish-based. The work of J.T. Gilbert has provided a traditional and most useful starting point for generations of local historians exploring Dublin's past.[1] Apart from Gilbert, a number of other important general introductions have appeared over the years,[2] most notable being F.E. Ball's *History of the county of Dublin* (6 vols, Dublin, 1902–6), which provides a detailed contemporary description of Dublin's suburbs at the beginning of the twentieth-century. However, because of the unique circumstances of Dublin, as the metropolis and centre of political power in Ireland for centuries, much of what has been written about it has concentrated on the urban character. This is particularly true in the sphere of social history where most work relating to public health and housing has tended to concentrate on the municipality and the well documented 'tenement question'[3] leaving areas beyond the municipal boundary receiving little attention. Because the 'slum question' in rural Dublin has received such scant attention from historians, this pamphlet aims to shed some light on an important, yet neglected aspect of Dublin's historical experience.

In the sphere of public health and housing, relevant legislation was implemented by the poor law commissioners, who after 1872 became the Local Government Board. From the point of view of this particular study,[4] the most important work undertaken by the Local Government Board was that carried out by the boards of guardians. These boards looked after the day-to-day running of the 'poor law union' and took detailed minutes of their weekly meetings. The richest source of material from which this study draws are the guardians' minute books. Much valuable information may be gleaned from these minutes such as sanitary officers' reports on the maintenance and upkeep of sewers and drains, the checking of dairy-yards and shops for unsound foods, the abatement of public nuisances and the cleansing and disinfection of houses declared to be 'unfit for human habitation'. When reading through these minutes the intensity and scale of such problems can at times be quite striking. Take for example the residents of Lower Kimmage referred to in a report by Dr Henry Davy, medical officer of health for Rathfarnham, drawn up in 1898:

> I have inspected the water as supplied to the residents of the Quarries Lower Kimmage and find there are sixty-six persons who derive their supply from an old quarry hole in the vicinity, into which drainage from pigsties and other filth are emptied, the water appears to be discoloured with organic matter.[5]

The raw content of such entries clearly demonstrates the value of these documents as an historical source. In the sphere of housing, progress on the erection and maintenance of cottages under the Labourers' Dwellings Acts also forms a large part of this material. Apart from the wealth of detail that can be found in these valuable progress reports, the guardians' minutes also provide harrowing insights into the extent of poverty and destitution then endured by the labouring classes of rural Dublin.

The first chapter sets the scene with a brief sketch of the geographical area under study. In this section the landscape is introduced to the reader, outlining its various contours from land quality and usage to building and settlement patterns. This chapter also looks at the background to the period in question by including a short note on the social climate of nineteenth-century Ireland including a brief history of the South Dublin Union itself. Here an attempt is made to demonstrate how a system originally designed to extend poor relief to the needy, evolved over a forty-year period into one whose main concern was the supervision of public health and housing matters. Management challenges and the local environment provide the theme for the second chapter. Here the issue of public health is approached from the practical standpoint of the local sanitary authority and its officers. In this chapter the reader is taken through the day-to-day duties of the sanitary officials as they endeavoured to clean up rural villages. Districts explored in this chapter include Rathfarnham, Clondalkin, Palmerstown, Tallaght, Terenure, Crumlin and Harold's Cross. Particular attention is given to Rathfarnham as this district was home to numerous outbreaks of fever.

The third chapter which deals with housing, looks firstly at the background to the Labourers' Dwellings Acts, examining the social and political implications that made the 1880s a more propitious time for the introduction of rural housing legislation. Also included is a detailed case study of an 1898 rural housing scheme in Clondalkin and Rathfarnham under the labourers' acts. This case depicts the many intricacies involved at a number of levels in erecting cottages for agricultural labourers, as the fastidious nature of such work is preserved in the original records. An important objective of the case study is to trace the changing nature of the role of the local authorities, unforeseen from the point of view of the drafted legislation. The relationship between traditional estate landlord and tenant has been thoroughly explored on many levels,[6] however, that of local authority as landlord and its subsequent relationship with tenants has yet to be considered. The fact of the local authority becoming a landlord itself therefore, seems vitally important and is very much in evidence.

The final chapter reflects on the monumental work carried out by the rural sanitary authorities of the South Dublin Union, and their overall impact on the making and remaking of the local place.

Geographical perspectives: the South Dublin Poor Law Union

The area of every poor law union, with the exception of those portions in the area which are included in the urban sanitary districts, shall form a rural sanitary district, and the guardians of the union shall, as such, be the rural sanitary authority.[1]

The poor law system introduced in 1838 was to become central to the future administration of local government in Ireland. Originally it was set up as a response to the wretched poverty, which itself was a result of agricultural depression following the Napoleonic Wars.[2] Its primary function therefore, was to administer poor relief through the workhouse. This however, would slowly change over the course of the century. In time the mechanics of the poor law system would replace that of the established grand jury system, taking on more and more duties as central government assumed responsibility for public health.[3]

Under this system the poor law commissioners, after 1872 the Local Government Board, were centrally appointed to oversee the Poor Relief (Ireland) Act, 1838.[4] They divided the country into 159 districts known as 'poor law unions', each of which was to be sub-divided into 'electoral divisions' of which the 'townland' was a further sub-division. Each electoral division returned elected representatives to serve on the 'board of guardians'.[5] These boards of guardians were therefore responsible for looking after the day-to-day running of the union. In order to stand for the office of guardian one had to meet certain property qualifications. Such qualifications were fixed by the Local Government Board according to the valuations it had placed on each electoral division. To minimise corruption and to ensure popular representation different qualifications were set for different electoral divisions.[6]

By the end of the 1860s, two decades after the Famine had passed, the poor law administration had long surpassed its original *raison d'être*, i.e. the supervision of poor relief. New legislation had empowered the guardians to act as burial boards and sewer authorities while also giving them responsibility for the removal of public nuisances. While this new legislation produced far-reaching results in the efforts being made to combat insanitary conditions in rural areas, the real milestone in the war against poverty and disease was the Public Health (Ireland) Act, 1878. Under this act each poor law union was to become the rural sanitary authority for its area. Along with this new

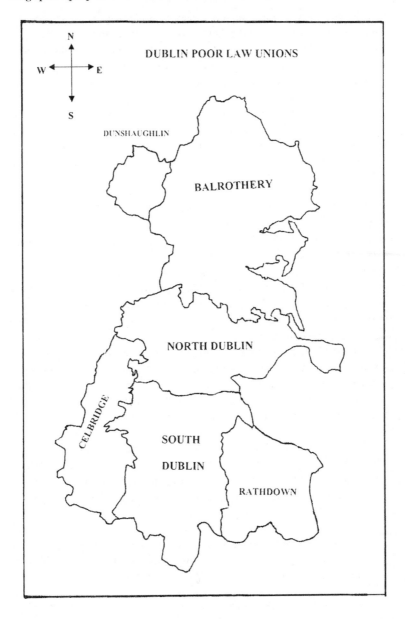

1. Dublin Poor Law Unions. Based on the general map of Ireland showing poor law union and electoral division boundaries (1891).

responsibility came an increase in the number of sanitary staff, each with the right to exercise authority in the destruction of unsound food, the supervision of dairy-yards and slaughter houses and the treatment of contagious diseases.[7] In summary, the poor law guardians, acting in their capacity as the rural sanitary authority, were given responsibility for all matters concerning public health in their areas.

The South Dublin Poor Law Union, with its headquarters on the site of the present day St James's Hospital, was declared on 6 June 1839. On the same day the neighbouring union of North Dublin had also been declared, its head-quarters situated across the Liffey on the site of what is now Grangegorman asylum. The two sites were chosen as they each contained institutions pre-viously associated with poor relief. These were the foundling hospital situated south of the river in James's Street, established in 1704, and the house of industry north of the river at Grangegorman.[8] Being the larger of the two unions, the South Dublin Union enclosed within its boundaries a population of 182,767 in 1839, compared to the North Dublin Union's 125,245.[9] By 1911 these figures had risen to 226,634 and 179,562 respectively.[10] The neigh-bouring unions of Balrothery, Dunshaughlin, Celbridge, Naas and Rathdown were formed in such a way as to encircle the two Dublin unions, thereby relieving them of undue pressure by assuming responsibility for Dublin's borderline townlands (Figure 1).

As an established body whose main purpose was to administer poor relief and deal with public health matters on a local basis, from the outset the guardians were not afraid to involve themselves in matters beyond their immediate agenda. This can be seen in the following motion, put to the board for consideration on 10 April 1901 by Mr William Sheridan:

> That we, the Guardians of the South Dublin Union, desire most respect-fully to urge upon his Majesty's attention the desirability of transferring two-thirds of the Royal Irish Constabulary to the Colonies or to Chinese territory, as such action would, we believe, be advantageous to the Empire and to Ireland by, in the first instance, relieving the taxpayers of a large annual impost which is at present spent on this force, whose duties might easily be performed by one-third of their number, and thus release such monies for technical education and to establish an industrial banking system throughout the country.[11]

A copy of this resolution was to be forwarded to 'His Most Gracious Majesty's Ministers, to the Chairman of the Irish Party, to the municipal bodies, to the county councils, to the rural district councils, and to the poor law boards throughout the country'. Despite its self-importance and vanity, this statement does seem to have been directed towards the good of the Empire. In January 1901 the South Dublin Union turned down an offer from the North Dublin

Union of amalgamating both unions. In their reply to the clerk of the North Dublin Union they reasoned that 'it would not be to the advantage of this union to become amalgamated with the North Dublin Union, and we respectfully decline the conference proposed on that subject'.[12] In September 1918 however, both unions did finally amalgamate by a sealed order of the Local Government Board, to become the Dublin Union. Five years later in November 1923, the board of guardians for the Dublin Union were dissolved to be replaced by three commissioners to administer the affairs of the union. These were Seamus MacLysaght, Chairman, Dr W.C. Dwyer and Mrs Jane Power.[13]

In 1881 the county of Dublin measured from north to south 32 miles and from east to west 18 miles, covering in total, an area of 226,895 acres. Of this land 103,698 acres were in pasture, 88,724 under tillage, 4,274 in plantations and 29,827 consisted of waste, bog and mountain.[14] Together this land made up the territories of the North Dublin, South Dublin, Balrothery and Rathdown poor law unions, and also included parts of the Celbridge and Dunshaughlin unions.

Table 1. Area, valuation and population of Dublin Poor Law Unions in 1881

Union	Acres	Valuation	Population
North Dublin	40,769	£365,293	142,981
South Dublin	48,089	£642,114	202,264
Balrothery	75,769	£95,392	19,067
Rathdown	61,514	£257,854	57,913

Source: Thom's Directory (1881, 1890).

As can be seen from Table 1, the South Dublin Union, although largest by far of the Dublin unions in terms of population, was only third largest in terms of acreage. This can be explained in that nine-tenths of this population was centred around the densely populated 'dispensary districts' of Meath Street, High Street, Peter Street, Canal Street, Donnybrook and Rathmines, leaving the more sparsely populated rural districts home to the remaining one-tenth, about 20,000 in number. Mostly rural dwellers, it is these individuals who make up the main community of interest for this study. Moving inland from east to west, the parishes inhabited by these people were Rathfarnham, Crumlin, Tallaght, Drimnagh, Palmerstown and Clondalkin. Apart from the lower reaches of Tallaght which extended southwards into the foothills of the Dublin mountains and formed the largest parish in the county, this was otherwise fertile land with numerous woollen, flour and paper mills scattered across the landscape. A feature of vital importance to this landscape and to the local economy was the watercourse of the River Dodder. The source from

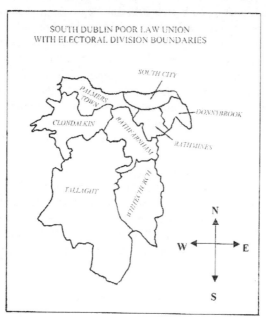

2. South Dublin Poor Law Union and Electoral Divisions. Based on the general map
of Ireland showing poor law union and electoral division boundaries (1891)

which numerous mills in the Tallaght district drew their power, John D'Alton
writes of this 'romantic river':

> The length of its course is but twelve miles, flowing, as is detailed at the
> particular localities, from the foot of Kippure, by Castlekelly and
> Templeogue, whence, running by Rathfarnham, Milltown, Clonskeagh,
> Donnybrook, and Ballsbridge, it discharges itself into the sea at Ringsend.
> Its early character is wild and boisterous, foaming amidst rocks, and
> usually swelled by mountain floods and showers, the close of its course,
> however, is gentle even to sluggishness.[15]

Because the River Dodder was prone to sewage contamination from various
sources, it is of immense importance to this study. This contamination was the
cause of innumerable disputes between the union guardians and the Rathmines
Township Commissioners. Examples of this friction can be seen in the following
chapter.

Spread out across the landscape of the South Dublin Union was a complex
jigsaw of townlands containing various estates, farmlands and small settlements
ranging in size from clusters of cabins to small but respectable villages. The
third chapter of this study which concentrates on housing, illustrates well how
the Labourers' Dwellings (Ireland) Acts, 1883–1919, implemented by the

guardians of the union, impacted greatly on the rural morphology of these townlands. Housing schemes were put in place all over the county so that by 1920 the mud cabin, so common a sight fifty years earlier, had been almost totally replaced by neat rows of slated brick cottages. In order to allow access to the main road for those living in the new cottages, a 'right of way' was necessary. Many of these passages are still visible today, having developed over the years into minor and secondary roadways. All of these improvements contributed in their own way towards changing the landscape.

The villages in this rural setting were simple and basic in their layout. Lacking the quaint charm and rustic sense of the English rural village, they possessed a unique practical charm all of their own. Standard buildings throughout most were the parish or 'established' church, the Roman Catholic church, the national and parochial school, and the Constabulary station. In the case of Clondalkin (Figure 3), which in 1890 consisted 'chiefly of one irregular street, of small but neatly built houses and cottages' (eighty-eight in all), the village also possessed almshouses for destitute widows, a Dorcas Institution, a Lying-in Hospital and a Dispensary.[16] Evidence of the ongoing change in these rural hamlets can be seen in the following quotation from Weston St John Joyce, as he compares the Clondalkin of 1912 to that which existed eighty-six years earlier:

> Making our way to Clondalkin, we enter that ancient village from the south, coming at once into view of the Round Tower on the left. Brewer in his *Beauties of Ireland* (1826), thus describes this place: 'The devious street is lined with the low cabins usual to the peasantry of this island, but with such as rank among the neatest of their ordinary dwellings'. Since that time, however, the village has been entirely altered and rebuilt, and the paper mills of Messrs. Kynoch, together with the neat cottages erected for the employees, give the place an appearance very different from that described by Brewer.[17]

With the ancient tower existing beside such modern structures as the paper mills, Clondalkin was a good example of past and present existing side by side. John D'Alton in his work of 1838, described well this harmony between two different worlds: 'The neat little village of Clondalkin presents itself; a smiling assemblage of cleanly cottages interspersed with the venerable remains of other days, all overshadowed by verdant groves'.[18]

The changes wrought in Clondalkin from 1880 to 1920 were substantial but not unique. Most of the union villages were marked out by the board of guardians as potential nuclei around which to build the new labourers' cottages in place of 'low cabins'. Tallaght, Rathfarnham, Palmerstown and Crumlin also changed over the years accommodating more and more houses as public health and housing standards rose during the period up to 1920. In

3. Clondalkin village, *c.* 1840, watercolour, artist unknown

his travels around Dublin in 1912, Weston St John Joyce had noted this
gradual change in a number of suburbs: 'Leaving Harold's Cross by the
Kimmage Road, at the south-western extremity of the Green, we almost
immediately emerge into the open country, though, indeed, new houses are
so rapidly springing up in this neighbourhood that it cannot hope to retain
much longer its rural character'. Also in the townland of Willbrook in
Rathfarnham (Figure 9), he noted the following: 'Presently we reach the new
Catholic church, where a turn to the right leads to Willbrook, now in a rather
decayed condition, but gradually being replaced by new dwellings built by the
rural district council'.[19]

Allied to this morphological change occurring in the villages, was a similar
change affecting the surrounding townlands. By way of compulsory purchase
the guardians bought up many fields and tracts of land in order to site the new
cottages being erected for agricultural labourers in the district. This action did
not always meet with the approval of the owners who in many cases objected.
In cases where the owner had good reason to object, the guardians would
usually settle for an alternative section of land belonging to the same person.
In most cases but not all, cottage building went ahead. This modernisation of
the countryside, although in a way destructive to the old landmarks and topy-
nyms, was nevertheless necessary because behind the cosmetic 'picturesqueness'

of the small villages and roadside cabins, lay the grim reality of poverty and disease. In the district of Rathfarnham in particular, numerous outbreaks of fever were reported during this period. The next chapter examines in detail the methods adopted by the guardians in order to tackle these problems of disease and deprivation among the rural community of the South Dublin Poor Law Union.

Environmental management: public health challenges

Local Government Board to assign to these [Sanitary officers and Superintendent officers of health] their respective duties and functions in the discovery or inspection or removal of nuisances, in the supply of pure water, in the making or repairing of sewers and drains, or generally aiding the administration of the sanitary laws in the district.[1]

The effectiveness of the sanitary authorities in improving public health conditions within the jurisdiction of the South Dublin Union is best examined through a study of the implementation of the Public Health (Ireland) Act, 1878. Under section 6 of this act the guardians of each poor law union became the rural sanitary authority for that area. During the period 1880 to 1920 such districts as Rathfarnham, Clondalkin, Crumlin, Tallaght and Terenure attracted particular attention from the rural sanitary authorities in south Dublin. By examining empirically the implementation of the public health act within these districts, insights into the practical effectiveness of the new legislation may be gained. Issues explored include the connection between contagious disease and the following related causes: contaminated water, inadequate sewage and drainage systems, lack of scavenging and cleansing facilities and the need for public nuisance removal.

The Rural Sanitary Authority came into existence in 1878 after the public health act of the same year issued the poor law guardians with responsibility for sanitary matters in rural districts. The establishment of this body was a vitally important step in the government's continuing attempts to attain a satisfactory public health strategy. Probably of most significance was the fact that it entailed a substantial increase in the number of sanitary staff available in each union. At the top of the scale the ultimate responsibility lay with the chief medical officer of health. In Dublin this position was first held by Dr Edward Mapother who retired in 1880 to be succeeded by Dr Charles Alexander Cameron, later to become Sir Charles Cameron (Figure 4). Dr Cameron filled this important role until 1912. In this position, he was responsible for much of the progress made by the rural sanitary authorities during this period. However of unrivalled importance throughout this campaign were the men and women who collectively made up the team of sanitary officers and sub-officers. Their duties were to monitor on a daily basis the sanitary conditions within their designated area. In upholding this

4. Sir Charles Alexander Cameron, chief medical officer of
health for Dublin, 1880–1912

responsibility each officer was required to carry out daily checks on business premises, family dwellings and public places, to ensure that standards of hygiene and cleanliness were being upheld. This entailed the examination of drains, water-closets, earth-closets, privies, ash-pits, cesspools, water courses and public places in general. If standards of hygiene were below the minimal acceptable level, officers were required to serve notice on the owner to have the problem rectified. Once notice had been served, where the problem persisted officers then had the authority to close down the premises in question. Most frequently targeted by these officers were the houses of the poor along with the numerous dairy-yards, shops, mills and laundries within the union districts. Officers were also required to write up reports on their daily observations with suggestions for remedying existing problems.

Wages of the sanitary officer and sanitary sub-officer varied according to the workload in his or her sanitary district. In 1901 the sanitary sub-officer for Clondalkin, John Anderson was given a £5 increase, making his salary £15 per annum 'owing to large district and arduous duties'.[2] Sanitary officers were required to undergo a competitive examination in 'sanitary science' before being appointed. After the Local Government (Ireland) Act, 1898, this examination was opened to women with the first lady sanitary sub-officer being appointed in 1899.[3] The inclusion of women onto the sanitary staff was due mainly to the influence of Dr Cameron who had appealed continuously on their behalf, as he firmly believed they would be most useful in educating women in proper sanitary habits, and the safe rearing of children.

In Dublin the rural sanitary authorities were not completely alone in their crusade to improve social conditions within the city and county. In 1878, the year they came into existence, another important body known as the Dublin Sanitary Association, was already six years old. This organization was set up immediately after the small-pox outbreak of 1871–2, largely through the efforts of Dr William Stokes.[4] The Dublin Sanitary Association had four key objectives:

1. To create an educated public opinion with regard to sanitary matters in general.
2. To direct the attention of the authorities and the public to those points in which the existing powers for the maintenance of the sanitary condition of the City are either not duly exercised or are inadequate, or in which the machinery at the disposal of the Sanitary Authorities is insufficient.
3. To watch the course of sanitary legislation on behalf of the public.
4. To form a body in which the public may have confidence, and through which they may, if necessary, act.[5]

The Dublin Sanitary Association was to become a very influential body over the next thirty years campaigning on many sanitary matters including sewage, water-supply, nuisance removal, scavenging and the notification of infectious disease.[6]

In the sphere of public health, the period from 1850 to 1900 is one of great discovery. It was during this period that French chemist, Louis Pasteur put forward his 'germ theory' on the spread of contagious disease. Pasteur believed that the spread of disease was caused by the growth of tiny micro-organisms called bacteria, and that specific diseases originated from specific bacterial organisms. Once these organisms were identified and isolated, major steps could then be taken in preventing their spread.[7] Prior to Pasteur's discovery most medical practitioners of the period had believed that contagious disease was transmitted by 'miasmatic' or air-borne causes, such as the breathing in of 'noxious vapours' emanating from open sewers and foul-smelling refuse. Although inaccurate, this concept of miasma and the methods deployed in its eradication, provided the sanitary authorities with an extremely effective strategy for promoting public health. As the medical profession in both Britain and Ireland was at first somewhat hesitant in accepting Pasteur's theory, the location and destruction of miasma and its causes remained the over-riding concern of the sanitary authorities in Ireland up to the 1890s. For example, as late as 1899, the head officer of health for Tallaght, Dr Poett was of the opinion that a 'foul-smelling' manure heap left in the yard of a lodging house in the village was 'most likely to cause an epidemic of fever'.[8] Evidence of this drive towards eradicating miasmic influences can be seen in much of the public health legislation of the time, particularly the Public Health (Ireland) Act, 1878.[9] This latter body of legislation placed much emphasis on such themes as sewage and drainage, water-supply, scavenging and cleansing, nuisance removal, and infectious disease. The assumption was that vapours and odours arising from open sewers, foul ash-pits, and domestic and industrial refuse, once airborne would pollute the atmosphere leading to the spread of contagious disease. The answer therefore, was to rid the community of these blights, and in so doing provide a healthier and safer environment in which to live. It was under these principles that the sanitary authorities set out their campaign in 1878.

Even as late as 1880, proper drainage systems were still urgently required in certain parts of rural Dublin. Despite the fact that the miasma theory was now rapidly losing favour in the medical world, the reality of 'foul stenches' and 'noxious odours' required decisive action. Also, apart from emitting unpleasant odours, open drains such as the one running along the Crumlin Road were also used for dumping animal carcasses such as 'dead pigs' and other types of refuse.[10] Whichever way one looked at it, the problem of open or blocked sewers, and undrained houses was serious.

Disputes and debates over the causes of sewage contamination frequently arose between the authorities and those parties being held responsible by the board. These could and did entail lengthy investigations by officials, sometimes

5. Loretto House, Rathfarnham, Dublin, *c.*1850, by G. Du Noyer

involving the use of third parties for legal advice. More often than not disputes of this nature would arise out of the reports of the sanitary officer for the area. One such case was the contamination of the water-supply at the Carmelite convent in Firhouse reported on 13 April 1891. The cause of the contamination was said to be the disposal of sewerage matter from two dairy-yards into the River Dodder which provided the convent with its water-supply. The contamination of any water source was deemed by the authorities to be a serious offence, particularly as it was becoming increasingly accepted that this was one of the major causes of the spread of cholera and typhoid. Notice was served on the occupiers to have the problem abated but to no avail.[11] Two weeks later on 24 April the streams at Firhouse were still being contaminated so the owners were presented with the following ultimatum: 'if the order to abate the nuisance be not carried out Mr. Fitzgerald [the board's solicitor] to take the necessary proceedings'. By 4 May of the same year the problem was still in existence and the solicitors were brought in for prosecution. This was a direct breach of section 19 of the Public Health (Ireland) Act, 1878, which demanded the purification of sewage before being discharged into streams.

Seven years later the Dodder was the subject of more complaint, this time lodged from the secretary of the Rathmines Township Commissioners to the South Dublin Union. The Commissioners believed that the Dodder was being polluted somewhere inside the territory of this union. This complaint prompted an immediate response from the sanitary authority entailing a number of inspections of the river bank. The first of these was made by Dr A. Croly, the medical officer of health for Rathfarnham. Dr Croly, having inspected the banks of the Dodder on the Rathfarnham side reported the following:

> There is no polluted stream running through Rathfarnham Castle grounds, but the sewer from Loretto Abbey which is laid under Mr. Blackburn's lands discharges its fluid contents into the Dodder near the Adelaide Convalescent House. By the terms of an injunction obtained from the Queen's Bench, the fluid contents of this sewer are purified to a fixed standard before entering the river.[12]

Figures 5 and 9 show Loretto Convent and its surrounding areas. Eight days later, on 30 August 1898 a second inspection of the river was carried out by the sanitary sub-officer, Mr Golden. Having inspected the area complained of by the commissioners, he found no pollution between Big Bridge, Rathfarnham and Orwell Bridge; however, on the county side over the Orwell Bridge he found 'two depots for depositing refuse down the slopes of the embankment'.[13] The report made by Golden stated the following:

> Mr. Francis Lyons whose property abuts this place, and whose bank lodge is on the river has his property up for sale and the lodge is occupied by Mr. Bernard Brady in his employment, and the slops and suds are discharged down the banks into the river from this house.[14]

As was so often the case however, the guilty party still refused to co-operate. On 19 September 1898 the board referred the matter to their solicitors and Mr Lyons was prosecuted under section 78 of the Public Health (Ireland) Act, 1878. This allowed for the sanitary authority to take whatever proceedings they deemed necessary 'for the purpose of protecting any watercourse wholly or partially within their jurisdiction from pollutions arising from sewage either within or without their district'.[15] This section was usually implemented in conjunction with the Pollution of Rivers Act, 1876.[16] The Rathmines Township Commissioners however, were still not satisfied. In a letter to the sanitary authority of the South Dublin Union they stated: 'It is not only the owners and occupiers of premises near the Dodder that are at fault but outsiders altogether'. They suggested notice boards be erected to caution persons from depositing rubbish in future.[17] Considering that fourteen years later Weston St John Joyce described the same portion of the Dodder banks (Figure 6) as 'extremely picturesque; a high wooded bank rises above the northern side, crowned by modern residences, while adjoining the road is the densely wooded demesne of Rathfarnham Castle',[18] it must be assumed that either some level of

6. River Dodder at Lord Ely's Gate, Rathfarnham, Dublin, artist unknown

progress was being made in the intervening years, or Joyce was basing his writings more on romance than reality.

Also confronting the authorities in the area of sewage and drainage was the problem of 'untrapped' sewers. Those along the road from Rathfarnham to Terenure were in a very poor state of disrepair, causing a 'foul smell' to arise therefrom.[19] This was said to be particularly injurious to health as the inhalation of sewer gas was still thought by many to be responsible for the spread of contagious disease.[20] The problem of foul smells arising from broken and untrapped sewers was commonplace throughout the union districts during this period. In an inspection of the houses of Tallaght village (Figure 7), carried out in 1899, it can be seen clearly just how urgent the need was for proper sewage and drainage facilities. In this inspection, Dr Poett had the following to say:

> In the village of Tallaght, which is built mostly on the left hand side of the road from Dublin I found all the cottages facing the road below the level of the pathway, consequently the rain comes in and renders the flooring damp. In Mr Barrett's yard there are two privies which accommodate fourteen persons, one of these was blocked, the other open. The latter was in a foul and disgusting state of filth; the level of

the floor of both is lower than the yard in which they are located, and consequently all the surface water of the yard flows into them.[21]

Dr Poett's report dramatically highlighted the dangers involved in the absence of an effective drainage system. However, in a similar inspection of thirteen cottages in the Grovefield district of the Crumlin Road, Dr Henry Davy, medical officer of health for Crumlin discovered the following circumstances:

> There appears to be no drain in the roadway in front of these cottages to carry off surface water, consequently there is always more or less stagnant water and road sweepings in this locality causing a nuisance injurious to health. Opposite Mr Richardson's Springfield House, there is a foul open drain from which there is a most offensive odour, this drain passes under the road joining one from Springfield cottages. The conjoined drains pass under Gibraltar cottage and open again into Mr Nierney's field finally discharging itself, after a distance of some hundred yards underneath the canal and eventually into the Camac River at Kilmainham.[22]

This problem of open drains was evident all over the union districts and required immediate attention. In most cases where they were found to cause a nuisance they were either disinfected with chloride of lime or roach lime before being cleaned out, or in the more urgent situations were replaced altogether with earthen pipe sewers.[23]

It is important not to lose sight of the interlinking nature between the various categories of public health. On the issue of water-supply, overlap into other categories is inevitable. The function of the sewage and drainage system was to ensure that sewage was being disposed of in such a way as to prevent the pollution of streams and rivers, therefore ensuring a proper supply of pure drinking water. That this did not always happen and therefore resulted in the contamination of water-supplies was one of the main reasons for the spread of cholera. This disease was known to spread most rapidly where sewage infected with the cholera *vibrio* seeped into the public water supply. This accounts for the way in which cholera outbreaks affected specific households and streets. If it was spread miasmically, why then was one street struck down by the disease while the neighbouring street escaped miraculously? Since the first European outbreak in 1831,[24] the unpredictability of cholera had baffled doctors for years, leading to the belief that the disease could take hold spontaneously for no explicable reasons. Gradually a pattern began to emerge where a common factor was found among the households of those suffering. The common factor was, of course, the source of their water-supply. Eventually it became clear that the water being consumed by those suffering was contaminated. The cause of death was usually dehydration and struck the victim down within three to four days.[25] This type of water contamination was also associated with the spread of enteric fever or 'typhoid' as it was commonly known.[26] Once the nature of cholera and typhoid is understood it becomes apparent why the authorities placed so much emphasis on the supply of pure drinking water.

In the early 1890s the local authorities met with enormous difficulties in repairing and maintaining pumps and wells. In 1891 in particular, there seems to have been no end to the difficulties experienced with this problem in Tallaght, Palmerstown, Clondalkin and Crumlin. The guardians' minutes for this year are littered throughout with references to pumps being 'out of repair'.[27] Tallaght and Palmerstown in particular seem to have been badly neglected by the authorities at this time. For months on end the pump at Palmerstown remained dry, giving locals no option but to improvise with whatever sources they found available, in this case a number of spring wells in the locality.[28] This situation continued for five months during which time the guardians had made an unsuccessful application to Dublin Corporation asking for a connection to the Kilmainham Township mains, in order to feed the Palmerstown wells. The Township's reason for non-co-operation was that they only possessed a four-inch drain, therefore making it impossible to feed the Palmerstown wells. Eventually, after much analysis of samples and measurements of sites it was decided to utilize an old spring-well in nearby Ballyfermot Lane as a source for the new pump at Lower Palmerstown.[29] Ironically because the Tallaght residents were deemed slightly better off in that they did possess a continuous supply of water, albeit 'muddy', they were neglected because their case was not viewed as urgent.

In fairness to union authorities however, they did work hard in attempting to ameliorate the short-comings of the water-supply. A lot of the time it was just a case of 'too much to do and not enough people to do it'. As a result residents frequently signed 'memorials' in order to get the attention of the guardians focused on their particular problem.[30] Some problems were so pathetic however that they just could not be ignored. Take for instance the residents of Lower Kimmage referred to in a report by Dr Davy, medical officer of health for Rathfarnham:

> I have inspected the water as supplied to the residents of the Quarries Lower Kimmage and find there are sixty-six persons who derive their supply from an old quarry hole in the vicinity, into which drainage from pigsties and other filth are emptied, the water appears to be discoloured with organic matter.[31]

This state of things was emphatically deemed 'injurious to health' and recommended remedies were quickly put in place. Although situations such as this were extreme, reports from the city analyst Sir Charles Cameron nevertheless revealed a poor quality water in most of the South Dublin Union throughout the early years of this study. As well as those places previously mentioned, the districts of Templeogue, Killininny and Firhouse were also below standard. Killininny, the old townland name for the area which now encompasses parts of the Old Bawn and Old Court housing estates, was situated south-east of Tallaght village. The water supply in this area was severely contaminated, being described as 'turbid and containing numerous particles (some of them micro-organisms) in suspension'. This well was ordered to be cleaned out by 'scraping' the sides, then emptying it and pumping it out for eight hours.[32] As in all minor catastrophes where somebody stands to benefit, the mounting problems facing the authorities in the maintenance and supply of water created a lucrative business in the trade of sinking and repairing wells. Mr Stephen Byrne of Newmarket, in the Liberties, was frequently called upon to carry out such work for the union. Costs depending on the size of the job could range from 5s. to £5.[33]

Most suburban villages at some stage experienced difficulty in maintaining a continued supply of clean water. When wells were not completely empty, in most cases they were spewing forth muddy water. Depending on resources, some areas were able to meet this problem head on by utilizing natural springs, as did the residents of Lower Palmerstown above. Others however, were less fortunate. It was in these less fortunate districts that authorities were compelled to show greater initiative. One such example was that of the sanitary officer for Howth in the North Dublin Union, Mr Morris. He came up with the rather enterprising idea of building concrete tanks in order to collect rainwater from the roofs of the Howth cottages. In June 1904 he reported:

> I think it would be well to collect portion of the roof water from the twenty-three cottages at Howth in concrete tanks above the ground level with an overflow from each tank, the tanks to stand four feet over the ground level. I do not like collecting rainwater where there is a good supply of well water which is not the case in Howth.

Morris also suggested placing a notice on each tank recommending the boiling of water before use 'except for washing'. Mr Morris' suggestion met with the approval of the council and a resolution was made to go ahead with the erection of such tanks on condition that they did not exceed £30.[34] As stated above, the subject of water-supply tends to spill over into other related categories. Two of the remaining categories to be dealt with in this chapter support this statement; nuisances reported were frequently related to water contamination, as was the spread of many contagious diseases.

The roadsides in front of many dwelling houses in the South Dublin Union were strewn with all sorts of litter and rubbish. Noxious odours emanating from a mixture of foul ash-pits and earth-closets, along with decaying food stuffs, made for a most unpleasant, and at times dangerous environment. Unlike their urban neighbours in Dublin Corporation who employed a cleansing committee under section 52 of the Public Health (Ireland) Act, 1878, the rural authorities of north and south Dublin opted for local householder responsibility as permitted under section 54 of the act:

> Where the sanitary authority do not themselves undertake or contract for –
> The cleansing of footways and pavements adjoining any premises,
> The removal of house refuse from any premises,
> The cleansing of earth-closets, privies, ash-pits, and cesspools belonging to any premises,
> They may make bye-laws imposing the duty of such cleansing or removal, at such intervals as they think fit, on the occupier of any such premises.

The authorities relied upon the police to enforce this regulation. In June 1891 the attention of the police was called to the 'filthy state of the street or roadway in the village of Tallaght (Figure 7), and that they be requested to prevent the practice of throwing refuse thereupon by the summoning of offenders'.[35]

The description of the cottages in Rafter's Lane, Crumlin Road, occupied by the tenants of Mr Cower's Inchicore Railway Works is typical of the scene in many of these rural pockets scattered about the county. According to Dr Henry Davy this was caused by 'accumulations of foul-smelling manure, decayed vegetables, rags and other refuse in front of the cottages'.[36] In nearby Walkinstown, another lane was described as being in a 'filthy state almost a swamp, full of mud and deep ruts, with emptying of ash-pits, decaying vegetables etc., causing a nuisance injurious to health'.[37] Of little consolation to the union authorities, was the fact that for their neighbours across the Liffey, things were no better. In Blanchardstown the cottages on the street leading to the chapel were described as being 'in a tumble down condition with props in front and all house refuse and filth thrown out in front by the occupiers'.[38]

It was not until the turn of the century that the question of scavenging began to receive serious attention from the sanitary authorities in north and south county Dublin. By this time of course, the previous 'rural sanitary authorities' had been made the 'rural district councils' as a result of the new county council system introduced in the Local Government (Ireland) Act, 1898. One of the major reasons for this intensification of the scavenging question was the rapid growth of the Terenure district and the subsequent deterioration that accompanied this growth. A classic feature of the urban slum in Dublin was the maze of back-street alleys, lanes and courts that provided a hotbed for the incubation and growth of disease. It was here that the waste and slops of multitudinous tenements and business premises were dumped. In Terenure the geographical layout was similar to these urban slums

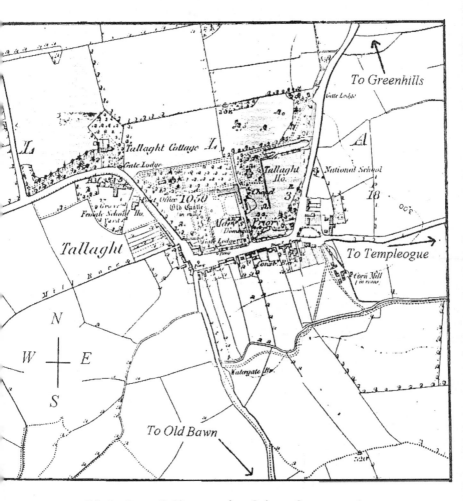

7. Tallaght, County Dublin, extract from Ordnance Survey 1:10,560, sheets 21, 22 revision of 1871, 1869. Permit No MP001501

but on a smaller scale. This urbanised layout is clearly visible in Figure 8. The areas around Westfield Lane and Farrell's Lane, both in Terenure, were good examples of these semi-urban, semi-rural slums in the union districts. In Westfield Lane the yard of Kennilworth laundry was described by Dr Henry Davy as being flooded due to the drainpipes being 'choked'. The lane itself he found 'in a frightful state, being full of mud and filth'.[39] In Farrell's Lane complaints were made of defective sewers improperly trapped and dirty and dilapidated privies and full ash-pits. The cottages were said to be in a 'filthy

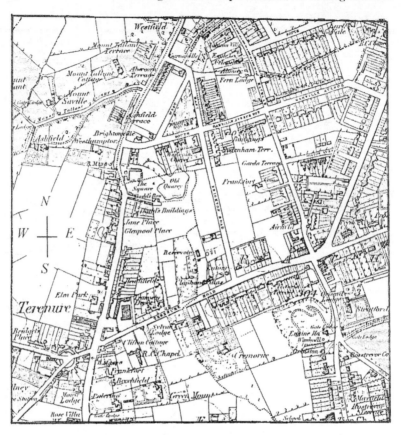

8. Terenure, Dublin, extract from Ordnance Survey 1:10,560, sheet 22, revision of 1869. Permit No MP001501

state' with 'black walls' and 'bad and broken up earthen floors, same being unfit for human habitation'.[40] In accordance with section 54 of the Public Health (Ireland) Act, 1878, notice was served on the receivers and occupiers of all these premises to carry out the specified remedies themselves.

Of even greater concern than the Westfield Lane and Farrell's Lane districts, were the notorious 'slum' areas of Dodd's Row, Janeville, Westhampton Place, Glenpool Cottages, Healy's Lane, Howard's Lane and Walker's Row. These areas, also situated in the Terenure district, had been reported consistently by the local sanitary officers in the years leading up to 1900. By 1900 however, the situation had grown so serious that they were submitted by the sanitary authorities, to a meeting of the Dublin Sanitary Association. In a follow on report by the Dublin Sanitary Association it was found that a number of old tenement houses in the aforementioned districts were without rears, consequently the privies were situated in front of the houses, quite close to the Harold's Cross Road (Figure 8). Several of these privies were said to be in a filthy state, and until a regular system of scavenging could be carried out for the removal of the refuse, it would be very difficult to keep them continuously clean.[41] The following month recommendations were made for scavenging carts 'to improve the situation at Healy's Lane, Howard's Lane and Glenpool Cottages'.[42] In this new endeavour to cleanse and tidy the streets, the authorities sought advice from the Rathmines and Rathgar Urban District Council. In a letter to the South Dublin Union from J.P. Fawcett, Clerk of the Rathmines and Rathgar Urban District Council, it was stated that 'with reference to domestic scavenging, some years ago the then [Rathmines] commissioners adopted a system of ashbins supplied to householders at a little over cost price, and for a fee of 5s. per annum, contents were removed daily'. What Terenure required was a similar system, however the more rural districts such as Clondalkin, Rathfarnham, Crumlin and Tallaght would have to wait a while longer for such services.

Under section 107 of the Public Health (Ireland) Act, 1878, the expression 'nuisance' was given a very broad definition. In this act the term nuisance applied to any premises, pool, ditch, gutter, watercourse, privy, urinal, cesspool, drain or ash-pit in such a state as to be 'injurious to health'; any overcrowded house, or any animal so kept as to be injurious to health; any accumulation or deposit injurious to health; any factory not properly ventilated 'so as to render harmless as far as practicable any gases generated'; and finally, any chimney, fireplace or furnace 'sending forward black smoke in such a quantity as to be a nuisance'.[43] Consequently the focus on public nuisances and their removal occupied a great many hours in the sanitary officer's already busy schedule.

Apart from the major problems of water contamination, open sewers, and filth accumulation resulting from various causes, hundreds of minor incidents such as defective chimneys, full and foul ash-pits and earth-closets, the dumping of animal carcasses in public places and the occurrence of 'effluvium' pervading neighbourhoods were also reported or discovered by the sanitary officer on a weekly basis. In areas such as Dodd's Row and Farrell's Lane in Terenure (Figure 8), Rafter's Lane in Crumlin, and Edmonstown and Rathfarnham villages, the ever-present occurrence of public nuisances was an ongoing headache for the local sanitary officer involved. Nevertheless they invariably rose to the task with dedication and professionalism. Throughout the period from 1890 to 1910, dairy-yards, and in particular those situated in the Rathfarnham district electoral division were found to be in a very poor state, well below the acceptable level of hygiene. This was due to various incidents, most of which fall into the broad category of 'nuisances'.

In response to a letter of the 25 April 1893, by Sister Mary Gabriel of the Carmelite Convent in Firhouse, and complaining of an 'effluvium' from a nearby dairy-yard 'which pervades the convent grounds', Dr Joseph James Byrne, sanitary officer for the area, visited the yard to find the cause of the complaint. Dr Byrne reported:

> I visited this yard and found there was an accumulation of manure, which evidently had remained there a long time, and was quite decomposed, emitting a foul stench when disturbed by a man who was in the act of carting it away. At the back of the cow shed not many yards from the road are three pits made to receive the urine from the cows (about 25 in number). These pits contained faecal matter about two feet deep from which arose a most disgusting smell. This with the manure heap was quite enough to poison the atmosphere of the convent when the wind blew in that direction.[44]

As mentioned earlier, although the medical profession was beginning to prove the fallibility of the miasma theory, sanitary officers in Ireland were still adhering to its principles as late as 1900. Consequently, the presence in the atmosphere of the effluvium mentioned above would definitely have been blamed in part for the occurrence of disease within the vicinity of the Firhouse convent. In this particular case the recommended remedy to abate the nuisance was to construct a purposely-built tank to receive the urine from the cows. This would be kept in the dairy-yard throughout the winter and emptied at stated intervals.[45]

Two months later another nuisance was complained of near the infamous slum area of Dodd's Row, discussed above. This nuisance situated on a property belonging to a Mr Townsend consisted of a filthy drain at the back of a local dairy-yard, which ran close to the wall of a number of cottages in Dodd's Row. After careful inspection it was concluded by Dr Joseph Graham Byrne, consulting sanitary officer for the Terenure district, that the cause of the nuisance was down to three sources. Firstly, from the condition of the dairy-yard where the urine and other fluid matters of the cows flowed into the drain, secondly, from the deposit of refuse on the land of Mr Townsend by the Rathmines Commissioners, and thirdly, 'but more remotely', by the privies used by the tenants of the cottages in Dodd's Row. This particular incident demonstrates among other things, the political astuteness necessary for successfully administering public health services at the local level. In order to abate the nuisance it would be necessary to have the dairy-yard properly drained with connections to the main sewer, which in this case was the Rathmines sewer. In order to have this done, permission would have to be granted by the Rathmines Commissioners, who themselves were partly responsible for the problem originating in the first place. Dr Byrne recommended that 'the Rathmines Commissioners should be prevented from depositing any material except dry earth in the field for the future, but, if permission is given to use the sewer, I would not insist on this'.[46] Concerning the privies in front of Dodd's Row, the problem here was drainage. With no water-supply available, the possibility of draining them into Dodd's Row itself was ruled out as the pipes would eventually become choked and end up causing a greater nuisance than the one originally complained of. The only remedy that Dr Byrne could suggest was that the privies be removed and the same number of privies be placed behind the cottages. These privies would have to be cleaned out twice a month, or every four weeks according to the amount of accumulation, and using as far as possible the dry-earth system.[47]

Several years later in 1900 the Rathmines Commissioners (now the Rathmines Urban Council) were once again found guilty of depositing rubbish inside the territories of the South Dublin Union. From May to October the authorities' attention had been called to the dumping of rubbish in the quarry holes in Lower Kimmage. Dr Henry Davy having inspected the area, reported the holes to be filled with 'decaying animal and vegetable matter, old rotten boots, cabbage stalks, rags, filthy paper etc., the odour from which is most offensive'. This, he said was a nuisance and injurious to the health of the neighbourhood, nevertheless it continued until October when the Rathmines Council were eventually found to be responsible. Recommendations were made to have signs put up to caution people against throwing refuse in the quarries, and also to cover the existing refuse with six inches of 'quick lime' and one foot of earth.

In most cases nuisances were reported to the authorities because they posed a threat to the health of the surrounding community. However, in the Public Health (Ireland) Act, 1878, such a threat was not strictly necessary for defining a nuisance. In section 107 of this act, part one states that 'any premises in such a state as to be a nuisance or injurious to health shall be deemed to be a nuisance liable to be dealt with summarily in manner provided by this act'. This was then footnoted with the following:

> The nuisances referred to in this section *need* not be injurious to health as well. Some of them can hardly exist without being injurious to health, but others may cause inconvenience, and interfere with the comfort of living, without being injurious to health.

Numerous unoccupied houses in the Rathfarnham district fell into this category of nuisance. In Edmonstown it was reported that such houses were becoming a source of nuisance to the neighbouring dwellings, 'being without doors or windows they are used for all purposes including the harbouring of tramps'. Recommendations were made for their closure.[48] Another such refuge for unsavoury characters was 'Cardiff's Cottage' in the village of Fox and Geese, in Clondalkin. This premises was reported to the authorities by a concerned resident, Mr V.P. O'Callaghan, as being 'nightly occupied by highway robbers.' Having applied to have the cottage demolished O'Callaghan went on to say that 'on Thursday morning last at about four o'clock p.m. four men occupied the ruin and left it singly, one in each of the milk carts for Dublin'.[49] Situated just off the main Dublin to Naas highway, derelict buildings such as this would have been a haven for brigands and highwayman awaiting the passing gentry on their way to and from Dublin.

Demolition of derelict buildings was not always necessary. If at all possible such premises would be put to other uses. In Church Lane in Rathfarnham, a cottage previously occupied by a Mrs Dunne and her family of four was deemed to be unfit for habitation as it consisted of only one room, and the family had all been ill since occupying it. Recommendations were made by Dr Winder the local sanitary officer to have the cottage closed up. However, not far from this cottage was the terminus of the Electrical Tramway at Rathfarnham and owing to lack of privy accommodation for the tramway conductors and drivers at the terminus, they were 'forced to commit a nuisance in Church Lane'. Dr Winder recommended the Tramway Company be made to provide a waiting room with accommodation for the men, and suggested the cottage previously occupied by Mrs Dunne and her family to be made into a privy and connected to a main sewer for this purpose.[50]

Environmental problems were certainly central to the improvement of public health but the control of infectious diseases presented an even greater challenge. In 1880, the opening year of this study, Dublin city and county was still reeling from the small pox epidemic of 1878–9. The epidemic swept through Dublin despite strenuous efforts on various sides to prevent its outbreak. In the summer of 1873 when cholera had broken out in a number of European ports and there seemed imminent danger that it might be imported into some of the ports in the United Kingdom, the guardians of the North and South Dublin Unions took joint steps to provide a special cholera hospital situated near the mouth of the River Liffey in Dublin Bay. The idea was to intercept any cases of cholera which might arrive in the port in foreign ships. As the site chosen for the hospital was next to the Pigeon House Fort, the military objected and an alternative floating hospital was constructed instead. Fortunately cholera did not arrive in this particular instance so the new floating hospital was never tested. Nevertheless the strategy was approved of and the new hospital was kept on, eventually to become known as the Port Hospital Ship.[51]

An incident concerning the Port Hospital Ship which occurred in May 1883 demonstrates the effectiveness of the ship in preventing the occurrence of possible outbreaks. A ship called the *Ardmore*, which had just arrived back from Riga, was reported to have a sailor on board suffering from small pox. The incident was reported to Dr Burns, consulting sanitary officer with the South Dublin Union, who immediately had the sailor transferred to the Port

Hospital Ship, *Prudence*, and requested a nurse, medicine and 'medical comforts' to be sent as soon as possible. Nurse Jane O'Reilly who had served at the Kilmainham small pox hospital during the epidemic of 1878–9 was promptly sent along. Next the *Ardmore* was placed in quarantine and disinfected, while the remainder of the crew were vaccinated. The patient was then to be looked after by a medical officer, Dr Finlay, as it was agreed that as little communication as possible should be held with the shore. For his troubles, Dr Finlay received the sum of one guinea per day. After one week of care the patient was reported by Dr Finlay to be improving.[52] In this particular instance because the correct precautions were taken immediately, a potential disaster was nipped in the bud.

The Port Hospital Ship was to prove over the years an effective, but not foolproof means of preventing foreign epidemics entering the country. Nevertheless it was not alone in this task. Since 1872 the Dublin Sanitary Association had been keeping a watchful eye on the progress of small pox and cholera as both diseases raged throughout Europe. Prior to the 1878 outbreak they had 'been watching with great anxiety' the progress of small pox in the large towns of England where it had assumed the form of a serious epidemic. As these towns were in daily communication with Dublin, the committee of the Dublin Sanitary Association thought it right to 'warn their fellow citizens of the danger with which they were now threatened'. In order to do this they produced a public placard which stated the following:

> Small pox is an extremely catching or infectious disease, and is easily carried by clothing or anything which has been in contact with the sick. It is therefore necessary that all clothing which has been in contact with persons suffering from small pox should be either disinfected or destroyed.[53]

When the epidemic did strike in 1878 the Dublin Sanitary Association communicated regularly with the two Dublin unions. In a letter to the clerk of the South Dublin Union in 1878, the assistant secretary of the Dublin Sanitary Association wrote the following:

> Sir, – I am directed to ask you to be so good as to bring under the notice of the Board of Guardians of the South Dublin Union, the increasing prevalence of Small-pox in this city, and to suggest that immediate steps be taken to appraise the inhabitants of your Board's District of the spread of the disease and of the danger likely to arise from non-vaccination.[54]

Not to be outdone, the clerk of the South Dublin Union in his reply stated that the South Dublin Union 'take most stringent and effective measures to carry into operation the provisions of the compulsory Vaccination Acts'.[55] However stringent the measures were, isolated cases were frequently reported to the authorities throughout the period from 1880 to 1910. Such cases however, were not limited to small pox. Killers such as typhoid, scarlet fever, tuberculosis and consumption, perhaps not as devastatingly effective as in urban areas, nevertheless took a firm hold in rural surroundings.

From the point of view of eradication, strenuous efforts were being made on all sides to contain these fevers. Dr Charles Cameron, medical superintendent officer of health for Dublin, and before him Dr Edward D. Mapother had carried out extensive research in the areas of contagious disease and its causes in Ireland. It was to these two individuals that the medical profession in Dublin owed a large amount of gratitude for its knowledge on fever epidemics. Of the five above-mentioned diseases, small pox, typhoid and scarlet fever were the most persistent within the territories of the South Dublin Union, particularly the Rathfarnham district which seemed to be a hotbed for fever at this time.

As early as 1865, Dr Mapother was busily engaged in researching and evaluating the sanitary provisions in rural Ireland in order to determine the need for relevant legislation.[56] From Dr Mapother's report it can be learned that even at this early stage contaminated water was generally accepted as a main factor in the cause and spread of typhoid, a theory now fully confirmed by modern medicine.[57] The following extract is taken from a paper which Dr Mapother read before the *Statistical and Social Inquiry Society of Ireland* in 1865:

> When it is remembered that diarrhoea, cholera, and typhoid fever are propagated by means of contaminated water, and that probably other diseases have a similar origin, no arguments are needed to prove that a supply of that requisite pure and above all suspicion is desirable for towns; yet every town I have mentioned tonight derives its supply from superficial wells or pumps, or from the rivers in towns, and such sources are rarely, if ever free from pollution.

The situation described here by Dr Mapother could have applied to most of the districts situated within the South Dublin Union. A particular incident referred to in the same paper relates to the inhabitants of a large house, nineteen in all, who had been attacked with typhoid fever from drinking water from a well situated within four yards of a cesspool. 'As is often the case with the most poisonous water', he stated, 'this specimen was beautifully sparkling, and had no bad taste or smell, but the microscope displayed crowds of organic forms'. If these individuals were deceived by the healthy appearance of the water, consider the unfortunate residents of the Quarries, Lower Kimmage. For these poor families who took their water from the drainage of a nearby pigsty, no such deception would have been possible.

Of all the towns and districts mentioned in this study, the Rathfarnham district including Edmonstown, Ballyboden and the village of Rathfarnham,

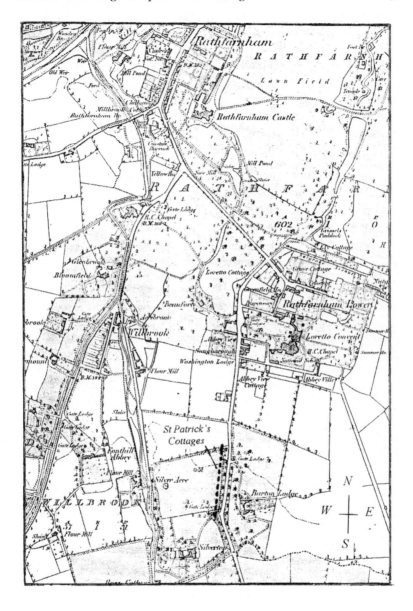

9. Rathfarnham, County Dublin, showing St Patrick's Cottages, extract from Ordnance Survey 1:10,560, sheet 22, revision of 1869. Permit No MP001501

suffered most from the spread of contagious disease. In the summer of 1891 numerous typhoid cases were reported in the Rathfarnham area.[58] When in one week four were reported in the same area, this prompted the authorities to order that 'the medical officer of health report as to the likelihood or possibility of the water used being contaminated'.[59] Two weeks later on 10 August 1891 the medical officer's report concluded that the typhoid did not arise from using impure water 'as in the first case they have Vartry water, and in the second case spring water'. What he did point to as a possible cause was the use by some families of an old pump in the area and recommended its replacement with a new fountain feeding of the existing Vartry supply.

In 1900 however, another spate of outbreaks occurred, this time the source was accurately traced to a number of dairy-yards in the locality. Probably due to inadequate sewage and drainage provisions, the milk was somehow becoming infected thereby facilitating the rapid spread of the disease to those who consumed the milk. In August a case of enteric fever (typhoid) was reported in the house of a Mr Campbell, 'The Ponds'. In this instance the patient was a child and was reported to be 'dangerously ill'. Mr Campbell was known to keep a dairy but stressed that 'no milk or milk vessels are kept in the house, the milk being sent out to the customers direct from the field where the cattle are grazing'. However, at the same time that Campbell's child had contracted the disease, so also had a member of the family of Simon Kenny, a labourer and dairy-man also of Rathfarnham.[60] A few months later the disease broke out again, this time in another Rathfarnham dairy-yard run by Mr Ambrose Langan.[61] Rathfarnham was rapidly becoming a problem area to the extent that the authorities, even in the city of Dublin, could not help but take notice. In his *Report upon the state of public health in the City of Dublin, 1909*, Sir Charles Cameron identified infected milk from a Rathfarnham dairy-yard as responsible for the spread of scarlet fever:

> Much of the milk consumed in Dublin comes from the country. In September and October, 1909, fifteen persons who had scarlet fever had used milk which had come from a dairy situated in the county of Dublin, a few miles distant from the city. On inquiry I found that a child residing in the house to which the dairy was attached had scarlet fever, which apparently had been contracted from one or other of two children affected with that disease who resided close to the dairy premises and were frequently in them.[62]

Although the actual district is not mentioned by name, Cameron does mention that Dr Croly, the medical officer of health for the district had taken 'prompt and vigorous action to prevent the disease from spreading', this in itself is enough to identify it as being Rathfarnham. Apart from typhoid and scarlet fever contracted mainly from contaminated dairy-yards, Rathfarnham also suffered from repeated outbreaks of small pox throughout the period of this study.

Clondalkin was also hit by these fevers but not to the same extent. In July 1898 Mr E.J. Redmond, Fox and Geese, and Patrick and Annie McGrath, Nangor Road were reported as 'suffering from scarlatina and occupying premises with others of same family not suffering'. Both parties refused to be removed to Cork Street Fever Hospital, therefore it was resolved that the families would be 'instructed in the Public Health (Ireland) Act, 1878, and after three weeks and a certificate of complete recovery, the habitations to be disinfected'.[63] Apart from the method of whitewashing mentioned above, another means of disinfecting premises was to burn within the building sulphuric candles; this was the method used in the case of Mr Redmond above, and also in the house of a Mr John Gannon of Ballyfermot.[64]

After disinfection of the actual premises, the Public Health (Ireland) Act, 1878 also required the total destruction of any bedding or clothing exposed to dangerous infections, with compensation being provided for the owners. This provision, reserved for cases of extremity, was diligently adhered to when dealing with typhoid, scarlatina and smallpox. Compensation usually ranged from about 12s. to £1 depending on the circumstances. The case of Mr John Watkins below, of Big Bridge, Rathfarnham, provides a good illustration of the details involved in the process of disinfection and compensation for losses. On 19 September 1898, Dr Croly, medical officer of health for the district, reported a case of scarlatina at Mr Watkins' house. In his report he informed the guardians that he would wait until the case had terminated before instructing the sanitary sub-officer to have the house and clothes disinfected. By 10 October the following month the sanitary sub-officer had carried out the required work and reported the following:

> In accordance with Dr Croly's instructions, [I] had the rooms occupied by John Watkins and family disinfected after scarlatina, and bedding also disinfected. The old paper on walls [has been] torn off and repapered. Chaff bed and tick, two old half blankets and a quantity of old rags [has been] destroyed by burning. Mr. Watkins is to be compensated amount of 12/6.[65]

Mr Watkins' case was further reviewed two weeks later with the recommendation of an additional 7s. 6d. to be paid on top of the original compensation. This brought the total up to roughly one pound. As is always the case, some individuals sought to rectify their losses by claiming for imaginary articles. One such person was Christopher Corcoran of Templeogue. Having had his house disinfected owing to a case of smallpox, and some articles burned, Mr Corcoran managed to stretch his claim to £5. This figure, far above the value of the articles destroyed, was reduced accordingly by the authorities in the final payment.[66]

Much common ground is shared between the various categories of public health. Lack of sanitary provisions in the areas of sewage and drainage, water-supply, scavenging and cleansing and nuisance removal all led ominously to the incubation and development of contagious disease in certain districts of County Dublin. Countless references to 'broken and untrapped' sewers omitting 'noxious odours' indicate conditions where disease was allowed to flourish. Contaminated water facilitated the spread of typhoid and other diseases in these areas, while the absence of proper nuisance removal and scavenging services contributed to the pollution of both air and water, thereby providing a hotbed for the growth of bacterial disease. Attempts to destroy the sources of 'miasma' by removing refuse and trapping sewers, however inaccurate this theory was, did nevertheless contribute to the improvement of public health standards. Reference has also been made to the especially urgent situation in Rathfarnham where numerous dairy-yards had to be closed to prevent the spread of typhoid and scarlet fever, not only in the immediate district, but also in the city of Dublin. Without the provisions of the Public Health (Ireland) Act, 1878, such already alarming conditions could only have deteriorated further.

This chapter has also exposed the early but significant stages of a new system that went on to create many changes in Irish rural life. The inhabitants of rural areas, having managed for years to remain detached from government bureaucracy, save for the workhouse and national schools system, were now beginning to find themselves more and more under the microscope. Government officials such as sanitary officers and medical officers of health were now entering their homes and becoming a very real part of their everyday lives. This state intervention on such a personal level became a regular feature of life in rural districts. This policy of intervention and its consequences, further extended with the advent of the Labourers' (Ireland) Acts, 1883–1919.

Rural housing reform: addressing the plight of the agricultural labourer

Sanitary neglect and carelessness as to the lives of the labouring poor must be remedied in some way. The hovels called labourer's dwellings in portions of the County Dublin, and in several other counties, are, to a great extent, a disgrace to civilization.[1]

In 1883 Ireland's first major public housing enterprise got under way through the implementation of the first of a series of acts known as the Labourers' Dwellings (Ireland) Acts, 1883–1919. These acts responded to an increased awareness, resulting from the successes of the Public Health (Ireland) Acts, 1874 and 1878, of the chronic living conditions endured by agricultural labourers and their families. As this chapter will show, some of the most sought after addresses in suburban Dublin today were formerly notorious for their dangerous and decrepit condition, most notable being the district of Rathfarnham. The background and operations carried out under these acts have been covered extensively in works by F.H.A. Aalen and Murray Fraser.[2] In these works however, both commentators tend to see the acts purely as the outcome of political campaigning and land agitation, therefore reducing the importance of the Public Health (Ireland) Act, 1878 as a contributory factor. As public health and housing are two inseparable issues, this chapter will therefore attempt to treat the labourers' acts as a logical progression of the Public Health (Ireland) Act, 1878, while at the same time acknowledging the social and political influences. Case studies from the Rathfarnham and Clondalkin districts provide fascinating insights into the trials and tribulations of enacting the housing legislation.

Newspapers, pamphlets, government inquiries and guardians' minute books clearly demonstrate how pressing the need was throughout the nineteenth-century for rural housing reform. Nevertheless the legislation required did not appear until the 1880s. For this reason it is necessary to be aware of the unique circumstances that made the 1880s a more propitious period for the introduction of the legislation.

The origins of the labourers' acts have been linked with good reason to the Irish land acts.[3] Ostensibly the legislation was introduced to ameliorate the pitiful living conditions of the agricultural labourer, but under the surface other factors helped to prepare the way for the introduction of the first act. The land acts had proved so favourable towards the tenant farmer at the expense of the landless labourer that some type of conciliation in favour of the latter was called for. This fact did not go unnoticed, and the Irish Parliamentary Party under the leadership of Charles Stewart Parnell set about attempting to bring both classes closer together. 'The challenge was to keep the labourers happy without showing so much concern for them as to alienate the farmers, who had a highly developed sense of proprietorial right when it came to their dealings with those below them in the economic order'.[4] This was accomplished by calling on the farmers to co-operate in extending the ranks of the Land League to accommodate labourers also. On 21 August 1882, speaking in Dublin, Parnell urged farmers in all parts of Ireland to band together in an attempt to help improve the wretched conditions of the landless labourer:

> Legislators recognize that their lot [the landless labourer] is unendurable, and that the clumsy legislation which has sought to remedy it must be altogether remodelled. Their privation, their patience, their unselfish national spirit are proclaimed everywhere, the national credit is pledged to securing for the Irish labourers some such amelioration in their own condition as they have so loyally striven to bring about in the condition of the tenant farmers.[5]

Having first stated the case of the labourer, Parnell then called on the farmers to join with him in attempting to firstly secure for them 'plots of ground and improved dwellings', and 'secondly to obtain such an alteration in the law as will further facilitate the acquirement of land by labourers and the building of suitable dwellings thereon'.[6] As rural conflict among farmers and labourers would have proved disastrous for constitutional nationalism, this unity between both classes was essential. Soon afterwards the Irish Parliamentary Party introduced into parliament a bill that would become the first labourers' act in 1883. The way was set to advance the cause of the agricultural labourer.

Murray Fraser suggests that while rural housing conditions in the poorest of English counties were every bit as bad as those of rural Ireland, the difference in rural Ireland 'was the determination of the Irish Party to win the landless labourers over to constitutional nationalism through the offer of better housing'.[7] While the Irish Parliamentary Party may be applauded for initiating the legislation, it was the Conservative policy of 'constructive unionism' that was responsible for sustaining the campaign into the next century. From 1893 to 1905 the Conservatives remained in power, during which time they cultivated a policy of state intervention in Irish social and economic reform in order to quell the nationalist appetite for home rule. One of the tactics of 'constructive unionism' was to amend existing legislation on rural housing with the introduction of the new labourers acts. It is true that the introduction and implementation of the acts certainly owes a great debt

10. Cabin near Finglass, attributed to Brocas family

to the constitutional efforts of the Irish Parliamentary Party and also the conciliatory policy of 'constructive unionism'. Notwithstanding this it must be stated that, had not the abysmal housing conditions of rural labourers first warranted such intervention, the manoeuvring of both political parties in this context would have been unnecessary.

Although effective measures were not taken until 1883 with the introduction of the first labourers' act, the need for rural housing reform had been recognized throughout the nineteenth-century from various quarters.[8] In 1882 D.B. King had described labourers' cabins in some parts of the south and west as being 'small mud huts one storey high, often with no floor, window or chimney'. In most cases the living areas were shared with animals: 'The inside is often much more like a very poor stable than a human habitation'.[9] *The Irish Builder* frequently published sympathetic articles calling for the improvement of the housing conditions of agricultural labourers. In these articles the moral as well as the social repercussions were recognized: 'Men who are obliged to vegetate in hovels all their lives cannot be expected to cultivate much manliness or independence, or reflect credit on their employers or rulers'.[10]

If such was the case throughout the country, the rural districts of County Dublin were no exception. In a North Dublin Union board of guardians meeting in October 1883, complaint was made that in Santry and Ballymun 'the labourers' dwellings were swimming in filth, the floors being ten inches under the level of the yards'.[11] These minute books provide sound testimony to the urgency of the problem in both Dublin unions, with countless applications by labourers to become tenants of the new union cottages. In the South Dublin Union the areas of Rathfarnham, Tallaght, Crumlin, Clondalkin and Palmerstown are all referred to. In the early 1900s the situation in the Rathfarnham electoral division was particularly poor and showing no signs of improvement. In the townland of Rockbrook the houses were described as being 'in a wretched state of repair, the roofs bad, walls dirty, doors broken, ground floors in a state of filth, upper floors worm eaten and full of holes'.[12] In Edmonstown many of the houses were unoccupied and without doors and windows, while in Abbeyview, the Ponds and Willbrook (Figure 9), houses were described as being in a 'tumble down condition and ready to fall in on the occupiers'.[13] The entry for June 1900 confirms the urgency of the problem in these districts:

> In order to facilitate and hasten the providing of suitable dwellings now so urgently required within the area of this district [Rathfarnham], it is resolved that Act 48 & 49 Vic., cap 77 section 16 and also section 12 of the Act of 1886 be adopted and acted upon by this Council.[14]

Section 16 of 48 & 49 Vic., cap 77 (the 1885 Labourers' Act) provided the sanitary authority with the power to 'purchase and put into repair any existing cottage which is in a bad state of repair'. Section 12 of the 1886 Labourers' Act provided for an extension of the powers of the guardians to purchase by way of compulsory order lands for the purpose of erecting labourers' cottages. By 1901 however, the situation had deteriorated so drastically that the Rural District Council requested the Local Government Board to confer urban powers on it for the Rathfarnham electoral division. The housing crisis in this part of the county had grown so serious that the council now considered it necessary for public health reasons 'that cottages should be erected for persons who do not come under the head of agricultural labourers'.[15] The problem had extended so far beyond this class that by the mid 1900s, the majority of working class people in Rathfarnham were in urgent need of housing. By securing for this division the status of 'urban district' the council would then have the power to erect artisan dwellings wherever required, thereby meeting the needs of a wider section of the community.

In Crumlin, where conditions were by no means as serious as in Rathfarnham, the council's attention was still nevertheless required. A detailed report by Dr Joseph Graham Byrne, consulting sanitary officer, and Dr Henry Davy, medical officer of health, reveals the conditions of thirteen cottages on the Crumlin road inhabited by agricultural labourers. These cottages belonged to a Mr Kearney of nearby Grovefield. The report warns of the threat to the health of the inhabitants as a result of open drains 'from which there is a most offensive odour'. Of the actual cottages themselves, the roofs were defective, the floors broken and uneven and the windows 'only one in each room about two feet by two feet, consequently there was a deficiency of light and ventilation'. Privy accommodation was also well below acceptable standards, consisting as it did of three outside lavatories in a 'dirty condition', for the use of the sixty-four persons who occupied the cottages. Generally, the cottages were said to be out of repair. As in the Rathfarnham case above, recommendations were made to invoke section 16 of the 1885 Labourers' Act and purchase the property. In order to render them fit for human habitation, suggested repairs included concreting the floors, enlarging the windows, repairing the doors, roofs and fireplaces where defective, and 'generally limewashing and painting them throughout'.[16] With regard to the privies they recommended that there should be at least six properly constructed lavatories (three for each sex) covered in from the weather, and that some of the cottages in the lane should have back doors communicating with a large yard in which one of the three existing privies was situated.[17]

Although the above extracts refer to a report carried out in Crumlin, the findings of this report could apply to numerous other rural districts in the South Dublin Union. In the village of Tallaght (Figure 7) all the cottages facing the main road were said to be below the level of the pathway causing the rain to come in and render the flooring damp. Inside, the houses were described as being 'dark, badly ventilated and quite unfit for human habitation' with a serious absence of privy accommodation. Of the two existing privies, one was blocked, the other said to be in a 'foul and disgusting state of filth'.[18] In Westfield Lane, Terenure, the cottages were described in 1898 as being out of repair with 'broken roofs, defective shoots, uneven and broken floors and the outhouses in a dilapidated state'.[19] As the weekly reports of the sanitary officers mounted, so too did the growing awareness of the need for rural housing reform, and as these needs became apparent the council reacted positively, albeit belatedly. This positive reaction can be seen in some of the suggestions for a new scheme in the townland of Ballymanaggin, Clondalkin in 1902. This scheme was to consist of both two storied and single storied cottages, some with four rooms and some with three. With regard to improvements, it was suggested that the cottages should have privies detached from the house and ash-pits provided; living rooms were to be at the gable ends, each with two windows; all windows to have up and down sashes; living room, shed and privy floors all to be granalithic instead of tiled; and all external woodwork in exposed positions to be omitted and substituted with brickwork.[20] Accepting that there was still a lot of work remaining to be done, standards had been upgraded considerably by the turn of the century.

The impact of these changes can be clearly demonstrated in a case study of the Rathfarnham and Clondalkin improvement scheme from 1898 to 1902.

The material used for this case study has been taken from the board of guardians' minutes for the South Dublin Union. Six separate volumes make up the period from 1898 to 1902 alone. Due to the scale of the present work it has not been feasible to consider the entire period from 1883 to 1920 when looking at the labourers' acts. Moreover, the South Dublin Union incorporated such vast territories within its boundaries that numerous improvement schemes were in operation at any given time. Taking these factors into account, the approach taken has been to isolate one specific housing scheme as the subject of a detailed case study.

In June 1898 the sanitary authority of the South Dublin Union acting under section 4 of the 1883 Labourers' Act, prepared an improvement scheme for the erection of forty-eight cottages in the electoral divisions of Rathfarnham and Clondalkin.[21] Proposed provisions for this scheme were as follows: in order to provide increased housing accommodation for agricultural labourers in these areas, the sanitary authorities proposed to take compulsorily, by way of absolute purchase, the lands and cottages described in Table 2. The total cost of the scheme with regard to acquisition of lands and premises, cost of building new cottages, repairing existing cottages, and legal, engineering, and incidental expenses was estimated at £7,600. The sanitary authority intended to carry the scheme into execution itself by borrowing from the commissioner of public works.

Table 2. Lands and cottages proposed to be taken compulsorily, by way of absolute purchase, and names of owners, lessees and occupiers interested therein

Townlands in which situated	Acreage A. R. P.	Owner	Lessee	Occupier
Rathfarnham	12. 0. 2.	M. Stephens	Andrew White	Andrew White
Rathfarnham	1. 0. 9.	Rep.'s of Thomas Donnelly diseased	William Keane	William Keane
Bluebell	2. 2. 0.	Lord Landsdown	Michael Flood	Michael Flood
Bushelloaf	8. 0. 0.	S.B. Rourke Floraville, Clondalkin	Christopher Hanlon	Christopher Hanlon
Robinhood	1. 0. 0.	Lord Landsdown	Margaret Short	Margaret Short

Source: F.C.C.A., SDU minutes BG 79/A4, 6 June 1898

Although initially prepared by the board of guardians in June 1898, the scheme was not approved by the Local Government Board until the 20 October 1898. Table 3 contains details of the provisional order relating to this scheme. Twenty-five copies of this order were forwarded by the South Dublin Union to the several persons interested, as required by the legislation.

Table 3. Provisional order for purchasing of lands to build cottages (under the Labourers' (Ireland) Acts) showing townlands where land is situated

Electoral Division	Townland	No. of cottages	Reference on OS Sheets
Clondalkin	Bluebell	6	1 on sheet 18
Clondalkin	Bushelloaf	16	3 on sheet 21
Clondalkin	Robinhood	2	4 on sheet 18
Rathfarnham	Rathfarnham	22	1 on sheet 22
Rathfarnham	Rathfarnham	2	2 on sheet 22

Source: F.C.C.A., SDU minutes BG 79/A4, 24 October 1898

After some delay the contract for the erection of the cottages was finally entered into on 21 February 1900. The contract itself was based on the plans and specifications of the Drogheda based firm of architects, A. Scott & Son, and the contractor was a Mr P.J. Hussey of Dundrum. The specifications were for forty-eight cottages, twenty-four in Rathfarnham and twenty-four in Clondalkin, all with half-acre garden plots and comprising three rooms in a single storey. The floors were to be of earthen tiles, the walls of eighteen-inch stone rubble and the roofs of slate, Killaloe slate in particular. These two latter specifications created endless difficulty for the contractor and the guardians when erecting the Clondalkin cottages. Stone paving was to be laid in the front of the cottages so as to provide footways, and the back doors were to have porches attached. On the negative side no ash-pits were provided and the privies were not as yet detached from the main building, which was then considered a health hazard. The duration of the contract was for a period of nine months. Figures 12 and 13 show these cottages in their present state, with the original Killaloe slate clearly visible.

Work carried out under this scheme was painfully slow. By 21 February 1900 when the contract was eventually entered into, the 'rural sanitary authority' had become the 'rural district council' under the provisions of the Local Government (Ireland) Act, 1898. Five months after the contract had originally been signed not one single cottage was complete. Although the Rathfarnham cottages were in the course of erection, work at Clondalkin had not yet commenced. Hussey's explanation for the delay was that although he signed the contract on 21 February, he did not get possession of the site until 5 March. Having gained possession he then encountered problems getting labour and materials, 'stone and slates' in particular. Aware that he would not

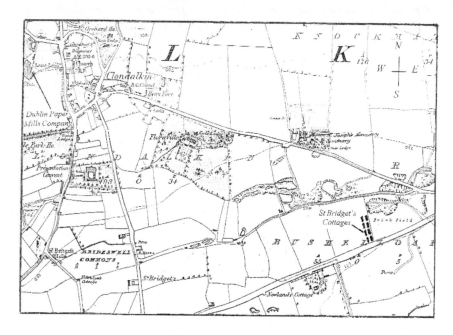

11. Clondalkin, County Dublin, showing St Bridget's Cottages, extract from Ordnance Survey 1:10,560, sheets 17, 21, revision of 1870, 1871. Permit No MP001501

make the nine-month deadline, Hussey applied for an extension arguing that 'nine months is not enough time as it only gives five days per cottage'.[22] It seems however from the evidence of the minutes, that work on the Clondalkin cottages did not commence until some time between January and May 1901, at least two months after the deadline had passed.

Hussey's difficulties in acquiring 'stone and slate' is verified throughout the minutes in an ongoing saga involving the 'Killaloe Slate Company'. By April 1900 progress on the Rathfarnham cottages was steady but protracted. The roofs were ready to be slated, but as it was learned that the Killaloe slates specified in the contract could not be acquired, it was decided by the council to use 'second quality Blue Bangor' instead. As soon as the decision was made to use a different slate, the Killaloe slates were suddenly made available and ready for use in the Rathfarnham cottages.

A lot of flexibility was required on the part of the council in adhering to the specifications of the contract. The contractor was having difficulty providing suitable paving stones for the footway in front of the Rathfarnham cottages and therefore wished to know if the council would consent to his substituting Portland cement concrete along the front of the houses, with stone kerbing and gravelled footway at the ends (Figure 13). The council agreed to this request provided it was carried out 'entirely to the satisfaction of the architect'.[23] Another deviation from the original contract was the omission of porches to the backdoors. By December 1900 the original nine-month period had expired and only fourteen of the twenty-four Rathfarnham cottages were complete. Mr Scott the architect, was particularly anxious to have these cottages occupied as soon as possible as 'the woodwork in newly erected houses gets seriously damaged by moisture when the houses are shut up after completion'.[24] By mid May 1901 the twenty-four Rathfarnham cottages were finally completed.

On 18 September 1900 Hussey was at last ready to seek permission of the proposed sites in Clondalkin, having first ensured that the Rathfarnham scheme had reached a satisfactory stage of progress. Figure 12 shows one of the eight blocks of two cottages situated in the townland of Bushelloaf, Clondalkin.[25] The first difficulty Hussey encountered was in attempting to acquire stone rubble for the walls. It was not a shortage of stone rubble that was the problem, but the hiring of labour to bring it in. It was now September and owing to the harvesting work labour was pretty scarce in the building industry. For this reason Hussey wished to know if the council would accept nine-inch brick walls instead of the eighteen-inch rubble walls proposed in the contract. The council asked the Local Government Board who in turn said they could not sanction 'such a radical change from the contract as it was not as warm or as dry as the eighteen-inch stone walls', however, 'the case might be different if fourteen-inch walls had been offered'.[26] A letter from Scott & Son, Architects dated 20 November 1900 made the final decision for the council:

> The contractor has now amended his application by proposing to build fourteen-inch brick walls, and to use best quality Harold's Cross or Dolphin's Barn bricks for the general facing with Durrow pressed brick dressings. We strongly recommend the council to accept the contractor's offer on this instance.[27]

This proposal received no objection from the Local Government Board and so fourteen-inch brick walls were used in the Clondalkin cottages. The task of roofing these cottages proved a lot more troublesome than it should have been, due mainly to the failure of the Killaloe Slate Company to co-operate with the contractor in supplying the slates. By May 1901 they had raised their price by 15s. per thousand 'apparently because they think the slates are bound to be used'. Disregarding this, the contractor was reluctant to use them any-way as they 'proved to be short grained and liable to damage in the winds'.[28] Taking this into account the council gave permission to use Welsh slate on 29 May 1901. Once again within a week the Killaloe Slate Company had agreed to deliver free of charge on the canal bank at Clondalkin, 'best blue' Killaloe slates at £16 per thousand. Seven weeks later however, there was still no sign of the promised slates. Hussey in a letter to the council stated, 'twelve cottages are ready for slating but slates have not yet arrived. Delays in supply of material retard the progress of the work'.[29] In this same letter Hussey stated that the sixteen cottages at Bushelloaf would be handed over by the end of October 1901, and the remaining eight two months later. This was not the case however, for as late as May 1902 the clerk of the union was still refusing to pay Hussey for completion of the cottages at Clondalkin. The final payment is recorded in the minutes of 18 June 1902 as follows: 'P.J. Hussey, Contractor, Dundrum, to be paid £38. 1s. 6d. amount of final instalment for building cottages at Clondalkin'.

Considering that the cottages, each with their own half-acre plot of land, were intended for agricultural labourers, it was important that this land be suitable for cultivation. With so much excavation taking place at the Rathfarnham sites, the master of the union had declared as early as August 1900 – having visited the site himself – that at least twelve inches of loam were to be laid down for the purposes of cultivation when the cottages were complete.[30] In January 1901 the Rathfarnham cottages were reaching their final stage of completion according to a letter from Scott & Son, Architects, to the council: 'Now that the houses are practically finished, and the levelling of the land attached nearly finished, it would be time to arrange about fencing, gates, right of way passes & c. at both sites (Rathfarnham 1 & 2)'.[31] Fencing of lands around these cottages was a major preoccupation for the council, particularly after the tenants moved in. Numerous complaints were lodged, and in fairness to the tenants the council did show a certain degree of reluctance in acting upon them.[32]

Applications for the tenancy of cottages would only be accepted from labourers living within the vicinity. The earlier the application was made, the better chance of success. The first application for the Rathfarnham cottages in August 1900, was for the number one site and came from two labourers living in the nearby Willbrook cottages. The area of Willbrook (Figure 9), was commented on by Weston St John Joyce in his travels around Dublin in 1912.[33] Other labourers were recommended by their employers or the local medical officer. James Murray of Rathfarnham was one such labourer, being recommended by the Rathfarnham medical officer, Dr A. Croly in December 1900. Mr Murray qualified as he was living in a single room deemed to be unfit for human habitation. Rent was fixed in November for these cottages at 2s. per week with tenants paying all taxes on their holdings. In choosing tenants for both the Rathfarnham and Clondalkin cottages, the following criteria were taken into account: 'as to whether the people are agricultural labourers or not, if they are living in unsanitary dwellings, and if they are of good character etc'.[34]

By 16 January 1901 most of the tenants for the Lower Rathfarnham cottages had been selected. A letter from the sanitary sub-officer, Mr Doyle, urging the council to allow those selected to move in as soon as possible reflects the poverty of their living conditions:

12. St Bridget's Cottages, Bushelloaf, Clondalkin, built 1902 (Photograph by F. Cullen)

> It would be a great blessing if the labourers now residing at Abbeyview, The Ponds and Loretto Lane, who have been selected as tenants of the labourers cottages at Rathfarnham were allowed to occupy them; their houses are very bad, a number falling in on the occupiers.[35]

These areas were located around the vicinity of Loretto Convent in Lower Rathfarnham (Figure 9). In answer to this request thirteen of the twenty-two cottages were occupied by 30 January 1901. These cottages were numbered one to twenty-two and named, in suitably nationalistic mode, 'St Patrick's Cottages'. The location of these cottages in the Silver Acre field west of Barton Lodge, can also be seen in Figure 9. The firm of Gleeson and O'Dea supplied the metal numbers and metal name-plate.[36] Continuing with the Irish saint theme, the sixteen cottages soon to follow at Bushelloaf, Clondalkin, were to be called St Bridget's Cottages. These cottages are marked south-east of Clondalkin village in Figure 11. Figures 12 and 13 show these cottages as they stand today. While the brickwork of many labourers' cottages has been hidden for years under numerous layers of paint, the present-day residents of

St Bridget's Cottages have made a conscious effort to restore these cottages back to their original rustic appearance.

As can be gathered from a close study of the 1883 Labourers' Act,[37] the completion of cottages by no means signalled the end of the council's involvement with the scheme. In fact one might say it was only just the beginning. Henceforward the council took on the, then inconceivable, role of 'landlord' to each individual tenant, as long as he or she occupied a labourer's cottage. From week to week multifarious complaints and requests were lodged with the council from the tenants of these cottages. By looking at the early stages of these tenancies, an insight can be gained into the process of getting a state-sponsored rural housing scheme up and running. Responsibility for the maintenance of such a scheme (through supervision of sanitary regulations, the repair of defects, rent collection etc.) rested to a large extent on the shoulders of the council. In the long run this system would lead to a new awareness within the rural community of sanitary standards, and also an unforeseen transformation in the role of the local authorities.

A large amount of vacant land surrounded St Patrick's Cottages and was the focus of much complaint from the tenants. The problem with this situation was that the land, not properly fenced, was used as a commons for the grazing of donkeys, horses and goats. As a result, the half-acre plots of land cultivated by the tenants were frequently trampled upon by animals roaming freely about. Four months after the tenants moved in, the council finally had this vacant land fenced off. The plan was to invite tenders for the grazing of the land on a seasonal basis.[38] This however did not bring about a permanent solution as the minutes later reveal. It seems that the tender accepted for the grazing of this land was that made by a Mr Donnelly who was however, the subject of further complaint, made by the owners of properties adjoining the land in question. The nature of these complaints was that Donnelly allowed the land to be used by a sports committee. As a result of this, football matches were played every Sunday afternoon thereby exposing residents to a great deal of 'bad language and indecencies'.[39] The following extract referring to a letter received by the council, and complaining of the same situation as that above, is valuable not so much for what it tells us about the football matches, but more importantly for what it reveals about the burden placed upon the council in having to conciliate all sides in matters of dispute:

S.H. Spencer, Milnrow, Rathfarnham.
Drawing attention to the fact that part of the vacant land [at] Saint Patrick's Cottages, Rathfarnham, overlooked by his dwelling house, is being used by a football club which plays matches on Sundays. A tournament is also to be held shortly. Requesting the council to take the necessary steps to have the disgusting and indecent conduct which takes place stopped before Sunday next![40]

13. No. 1 St Patrick's Cottages, Rathfarnham, built 1901 (Photograph by F. Cullen)

In contrast to these views expressed by Madden and Spencer, the parish priest and other local residents, expressing no objection to the use of the land for football matches, requested that the plot be preserved as a playground. Conflicting views such as these were frequently presented before the council for deliberation. Such deliberations required much dexterity on the council's part, particularly as their new responsibilities were now reaching into uncharted realms.

The above instances refer to the early stages of the tenancies of St Patrick's, and to a lesser extent, St Bridget's Cottages. Some of these tenancies would change after months, others after years, while some lasted a lifetime. Some cottages were to remain in the one family for generations being passed on from father to son or husband to wife, as in the case of No. 13 St Bridget's Cottages, occupied in 1902 by Mr Austin Cairncross and in 1998 by Mrs Alice Cairncross.[41] The fact that both sets of cottages are still standing today is primarily a testament to the quality of workmanship, but also a testament to the impact that just one aspect of local government would have on rural life in the new century. Over the years the council in its new role, would deal with countless situations involving the tenants of St Patrick's and St Bridget's Cottages.

It is difficult to recreate the vibrancy of tenant life during the period 1883 to 1920 and portray them as real people rather than just 'problems' in the guardian's minute books. Being poor and of the lowest class, these people struggled daily trying to make the best of their unfortunate circumstances. In many cases poverty and class were the only common ground they shared, possessing as they did a diversity of backgrounds and personalities. Whether noble of character or roguish by nature, they were a simple people with simple basic needs, who conducted their lives with whatever amount of dignity they could muster.

Great feats of solidarity were displayed among tenants in a number of instances. In December 1890 the tenants of the cottages at Clondalkin village found themselves in dispute with the owners of the nearby Dublin Paper Mills Company. This premises is marked in Figure 11 at the western side of Clondalkin village. The report of Mr R. Buckley, sanitary officer, states that 'the tenants of the Clondalkin village cottages have refused to pay their rents because the managers of the adjacent mill had kept some straw in their gardens'.[42] It seems the land allotted to the new union cottages had previously been used for storage purposes by the owners of the mill premises. As the mill owners continued to use the land for this purpose the tenants believed they were being denied the right to their own land. This caused them to vent their anger on the union authorities by refusing to pay their rents. While the guardians were in no mood to entertain such threatening tactics from the tenants, they did however issue their own threat to the mill owners to the effect that they would 'take proceedings against them unless the straw is removed forthwith'.[43] This marks the beginning of a long dispute between the tenants of the cottages and the owners of the mills. Like so many instances before and yet to come, the guardians, caught in the middle were expected to resolve the situation. After much deliberation, and refusal by the Local Government Board to allow the mill owners to purchase the cottages for business purposes, resolution was eventually reached in January 1892 with the Dublin Paper Mills Company agreeing to remove the straw and settle with the tenants for their losses. This outcome was important as it signified a victory for the ordinary labourer against the middle-class industrialist. As a tenant of the rural district council, the ordinary labourer was suddenly empowered in a previously unimaginable way. He or she could now make cautious demands, and with the help of their new landlords (the rural sanitary authority), could expect on occasion to achieve welcome results.

Even more militant than the Clondalkin tenants were those of the Killininny labourers' cottages in Tallaght. Having applied to the South Dublin Rural District Council for the job of removing a ditch situated in front of their cottages, the Killininny tenants were outraged when the decision was made to employ a local farmer instead. United in their anger, the tenants wrote the following threatening letter to the clerk of the union, Mr J.J. Byrne:

Dear Sir,

The tenants of the above cottages begs to ask why the removing of a ditch in front of cottages was given to Mr Patrick Byrne, dairyman and farmer, and the poor tenants left out, we all sent in our agreements and we were never offered anything, less or more we knew we would not get what we asked but we were offered nothing, it is not fair to give the removing of same to an independent man like Mr Byrne and all the poor tenants willing to remove the ditch, but no matter who comes to remove it they will get what Mr Byrne got if not worse, you will have to send an escort of police along with them, either that, or they leave it alone, kindly let us have one word or another. Whenever convenient we oblige.

Tenants of Killininny.[44]

What angered the tenants more than anything, was the fact that they had been completely ignored by the council. Had their application received some recognition, no matter how small, things might not have seemed so bad. Nevertheless, here is another fine example of the social advancement of this class of people over the 'almost three decade' period since the passing of the first labourers' act. Previously, such effrontery on the labourer's part, would have been unheard of when communicating with their social superiors.

Communication between tenants and guardians was constant. A continuous flow of letters arrived almost daily at union headquarters in James's Street. The following extracts come from a random selection of these letters received in the year 1911. Evidence of the varied backgrounds from which these people emerged can be seen in the contrasting styles of handwriting and levels of literacy. More importantly however, is the evidence of neglect on the council's part, where in some cases the requests of tenants were left unanswered for over a year. While there is no doubting the merits of the council's efforts to rectify the rural housing crisis in Dublin, the contents of these letters do, however, show that there was definite room for improvement. This fact would not have gone unnoticed by Mr Christopher Sherry of No. 1 Coldcut Cottages, Blackditch Road, Clondalkin. In October 1911 Mr Sherry wrote to the council as follows:

Dear Sir,

I wish respectfully to once more draw your attention to the shocking condition in which this cottage is at present. I may say at once that it is actually a great source of danger and the height of discomfort to myself and family. About twelve months ago I drew the attention of the Council to the miserable condition in which we were placed to face the severities of the winter and I think as a tenant of over nine years I should receive some little consideration. I was promised a range to try and prevent the awful smoking of the place but it has yet to come. And the gable end is in a deplorable condition, the coating of the walls falling around the floor from damp and want of proper plastering.

So now please I will once more appeal to you to have something done to remedy these conditions before the winter is set in upon us. Hoping you may be pleased to have it attended to at once.

> I remain Sir,
> Respectfully yours,
> Christopher Sherry.[45]

The complaint of faulty ranges and the subsequent problem of smoke and fumes was common among tenants, and as it qualified as a nuisance under the Public Health (Ireland) Act, 1878, it therefore warranted immediate attention. However immediate attention was not always forthcoming as Mr Sherry was to discover. Five weeks later with the situation as yet unchanged, he was forced to write for a third time:

> Dear Sir,
>   I respectfully beg to call your attention to the unhealthy conditions of living attached to the above cottage. I have written to the Secretary and Chairman of the County Council drawing their attention to same and it seems to tend to no purpose. I appealed to them to have it settled before the severity of winter would come down on myself and family. We are in the first place, practically smoked out of the place, and then to get rid of this we must open the door wide thereby exposing ourselves to all the inclemencies of wind and weather. A new range arrived some few weeks ago but it has lain on the floor untouched since and no one has been sent to put it up. If this was settled we might at least be spared some of the hardships. I am a tenant of the place over nine years and surely I am worth this trifling concession. Hoping you will see to this matter and have it righted.
>
> > I beg to remain Sir,
> > Respectfully yours,
> > Christopher Sherry.[46]

Mr Sherry's letter stands out as much for the dignified manner in which he approached the council, as for the actual problems with which he was faced. In contrast to Mr Sherry's letters, Mrs Mary Begg of No. 2 Riverside Cottages, Templeogue, confronted with similar difficulties, had this to say:

> Dear Mr Byrne,
>   Will you try and get us a range as we are blinde with smoke every day. I would be thankful to you, the chimley is very bad, the children is sick with the smoke, the doctor said it is the cause of the smoke. I hope you will do your best and get us a range.
>
> > I remain yours,
> > Mary Beg.[47]

The touching simplicity evident in Mrs Begg's letter reflects her lamentable circumstances. Apart from broken and missing ranges and other faults, in many cases families simply outgrew their cottage, resulting in six or seven adults sharing one bedroom. Facing such problems Eliza Naylor of Robinhood, Clondalkin, could foresee only one solution:

> Gentlemen,
>   I beg to ask that an additional room be built to my cottage, I have ten in family of grown up boys and girls, I have two small rooms and kitchen, the rooms hold only one large bed each. Sleeping accommodation is very cramped, I am over twenty years in this cottage, I don't think I am asking too much.
>   I am,
>   Respectfully yours,
>   Eliza Naylor.[48]

As overcrowding was now known to be both morally and physically unhealthy, it was particularly important that such problems were rectified. As many tenants faced similar problems to those of Mrs Naylor, the answer was to build both two-storied and single-storied cottages in union districts. By 1900 the authorities had already embarked on such a plan with many two-storied cottages being erected within the union, nevertheless, the real problem was one of supply and demand. With 15,092 cottages built country-wide in 1901, and a further 19,541 authorised, this went only a fraction of the way towards providing for the 258,000 agricultural labourers that were in existence.[49] As Nicholas Synnott, one of the few critics of the labourers' acts stated, 'to give a cottage and plot to every [labourer] would make the burden of local taxation unbearable'.[50] While such shortcomings on the council's part may appear trivial compared to their otherwise Trojan efforts, from the viewpoint of the individual tenant facing the winter with a leaking roof or a faulty range, they could be of immense importance.

By 31 March 1920 a total of 47,966 cottages had been built in Ireland under the Labourers' (Ireland) Acts, 1883–1919.[51] This figure is impressive by any standards as is acknowledged by most commentators.[52] In fact apart from Nicholas J. Synnott, few have attempted to criticize the work carried out under these acts.[53] As a result of the labourers' acts, the labouring classes in rural Dublin were given the opportunity to improve their social standing. No longer did they have to play second fiddle to the small farmers who had for so long enjoyed a far more acceptable social status. As tenants of the council, labourers suddenly found they were on an equal, and in many cases superior footing with that of the small farmer when it came to housing, a fact known only too well to Nicholas J. Synnott: 'Thousands of small farmers, whose own houses are far inferior to the new cottages, now bitterly complain of the injustice of paying for the accommodation of labourers who do not work for them'.[54] Apart from the imminent improvements of their living conditions, the agricultural labourers also found themselves in a stronger social position when it came to their dealings with those above them in the social pyramid. This can be seen in the Clondalkin tenants' dispute with the Dublin Paper Mills Company, and the Killininny tenants' dispute with the South Dublin Rural District Council.

Evidence has also been shown of the unique circumstances that developed from this transformation in the lives of the labouring classes. Agricultural labourers, many of whom still remembered the fraught relationship of landlord and tenant prior to the land acts of the 1880s and 1890s, were now having to adapt to a new and strange situation where the landlord was now a government body. In addition, after 1898 this body would be composed of democratically elected representatives, whose duty it was to look after the well being of their constituents. Perhaps the legacy of the labourers' acts can best be described as providing an epilogue to the nineteenth-century. As the housing conditions of the labouring classes improved, memories of post-Famine deprivation receded further and further into the background. Thanks to the labourers' acts, the twentieth-century held out real promise for the agricultural labourer.

Conclusion

By the end of the nineteenth century the great mystery as to what caused the spread of infectious disease had been solved. Many traditionalists, though not all, slowly relinquished their cherished belief in the theory of miasmatic causes, as the opposing theory of bacterial growth became more and more acceptable. In Ireland the fruits of Pasteur's discovery were now beginning to show as public health reformers declared war on filth in a determined effort to curb bacterial growth. As a result of this medical advancement, fevers such as typhus, small pox, scarlatina and cholera, while not totally eradicated, were at least now being contained. The importance of this breakthrough from a local point of view has been clearly demonstrated in the change it effected in the South Dublin Poor Law Union. While cholera was particularly rare in this union during the period from 1880 to 1920, the other zymotic diseases were quite prevalent in the early 1900s at least. If early attempts at eradication through the removal of miasma were misguided in theory, in practice however, they proved effective. For instance the act of removing effluvium and its sources such as open sewers and drains, did prove an unwitting but nevertheless effective method for limiting the cause of water contamination, an occurrence synonymous with the outbreak of fever within the union. If water contamination was the main source of fever, districts in which there were a large number of dairy-yards also suffered badly. Worst hit was the district electoral division of Rathfarnham, where its numerous dairy-yards provided conditions where fever was allowed to flourish. As a result of inadequate sewage and drainage facilities in these premises, contaminated milk became the agent for the dissemination of typhus and small pox throughout the district and beyond. Due to the provisions of the Public Health (Ireland) Act, 1878, the sanitary officers of the South Dublin Union, armed with a proper understanding of the nature and cause of these diseases, were by the close of the nineteenth century, well on their way to controlling them.

One of the strengths of the Public Health (Ireland) Act, 1878, was the way in which it increased awareness throughout the rural communities of matters such as personal hygiene and sanitary standards, therefore encouraging people to co-operate with officials and become actively involved in the improvement of their own living conditions. This however did lead to a qualitative change in the lives of the rural poor which involved regular dealings with government officials in a very immediate, even intimate way. Prior to 1878 this class had, to a certain extent, been excluded from the rest of society. Apart from the workhouse and national schools system they had had no previous dealings with government officials. With the arrival of the public health legislation however, the policy of state intervention extended into the homes of the rural population for the first time. With the advent of the labourers' acts in 1883 this intervention intensified, as the rent collector was now added to the growing number of government officials involved in the lives of the rural poor. By this time however, they had been well initiated into the machinery of state, and while this intervention may at first have seemed unwelcome, the obvious benefits that accompanied it such as clean drinking water and a slated brick cottage were enough to make any intrusion worthwhile.

With the advent of the rural housing legislation a new dimension was given to the already effective methods of containing disease. As public health and housing are two inseparable issues, the housing legislation was essential if the existing legislation was to achieve its true potential. The improvement schemes carried out in Dublin during this period were to have lasting effects on the lives of those lucky enough to become tenants. The Clondalkin and Rathfarnham case study demonstrates the positive effects of this state-sponsored housing for agricultural labourers. Here the intricate and often tangled arrangements involved in erecting cottages is quite apparent. If the initial legislation seemed complex to begin with, the actual process of implementing it was labyrinthine. Every step the guardians took was checked and double checked by the Local Government Board, including the proposed width of walls, the inclusion or omission of porches, what type of slates to use, should new houses be built or existing ones repaired, and how much money was to be spent by the guardians in the enactment of each particular scheme.

Not only did the erection of cottages improve the living conditions of labourers, it also contributed greatly to their social standing. As stated in the third chapter, a major unforeseen transformation had taken place in the status of the council whereby it now took on the role of landlord to each individual tenant. With memories of the notorious past relationships between landlord and tenant still fresh in the minds of the older generation, these people appreciated their newly acquired status. No longer were they at the mercy of a tyrannous landlord who could evict them whenever and for whatever reason suited, they were now protected by the State and as long as they avoided trouble and paid their rents they had nothing to fear. Not only were they secure in their new status as tenants to the council, they could also afford to be quite brash in their demands. A good example of this is seen where the tenants of the Clondalkin village cottages in 1892 won a long fought dispute with the powerful Dublin Paper Mills Company. This represented a significant victory for the labourer at the bottom of the social pyramid, against the powerful middle-class industrialist. For such a lowly class of people, this would have been unimaginable ten years earlier.

The new political and social changes that came about also had many repercussions for the council. As the third chapter has shown, the council was to frequently find itself in the middle of disputes between tenants and third parties. Some of these situations could reach bizarre proportions such as having to cancel football matches in order to placate local residents not even living in union cottages. The council was constantly called in to settle disputes between disgruntled tenants arguing over matters of trespass onto one another's land. In the majority of cases these arguments focussed on trespass by the neighbours' 'chickens' rather than by the neighbours themselves. If anything at all negative is to be said about the implementation of these acts, perhaps they may have been responsible for creating a 'culture of dependency', whereby the tenants became too dependent on the council to play the role of mediator in every little dispute that occurred. Also on the negative side, this chapter touched on another aspect of the council's dealings with its tenants, and one which is not generally recognized. From the evidence of a number of letters written from tenants to the council in 1911, there does seem to have been a certain amount of neglect on the council's part. In certain cases tenants were left waiting for up to one year for basic necessities and repairs to their cottage. While a heavy workload may be mentioned in the council's defence, one cannot excuse the fact of a labourer and his family having to endure the hardships of winter without the use of a simple range. Having said this of course, such pitfalls have to be measured with the long-term benefits the new system brought. Gone for good was the dilapidated cabin with its propped up walls, broken doors and mud-covered floors.

As this study draws to a close it is time to pause for a brief moment and reflect on the numerous events and changes that occurred in the sphere of public health during the period 1880–1920. As the old century ended, the thatched mud cabin, so common throughout the countryside right up to the 1880s, had been banished almost from sight in County Dublin. Areas such as Rathfarnham, Clondalkin, Terenure, Crumlin, Tallaght and Palmerstown were now beginning to feel the benefits of a tireless campaign of sanitary reform begun in earnest in 1878, and sustained right into the new century. Villages such as these began to thrive as the twentieth century progressed. Terenure, Harold's Cross and parts of Rathfarnham became more and more urbanised with many artisan rather than labourer's dwellings being built in these areas. Rent collectors and sanitary officers were commonplace in the villages and towns of the county by 1920, at which point such abominations as open sewers, full and foul ash-pits, and the common sight of rotten animal carcasses were rapidly becoming memories.

This much-needed change owes its foundations to the discovery by Monsieur Pasteur of bacteria, thereby pointing the rest of the medical world in the right direction. In Dublin such eminent practitioners as Dr Edward Mapother and Sir Charles Cameron were quick to apply the new knowledge to their own work, resulting in the rapid advancement of public health services both city-wide and county-wide. Of no less importance however, to the work of Doctors Mapother and Cameron, was that of the numerous ranks of dedicated sanitary officers and sub-officers on the ground level. These individuals were responsible for ensuring that sanitary regulations were being strictly adhered to, a task they performed commendably. By 1920, the closing year of this study, thanks to the co-operation and commitment of all personnel involved, the lifestyle of the labouring classes in the South Dublin Poor Law Union had been upgraded considerably.

Notes

ABBREVIATIONS

BG	Board of Guardians
DSA	Dublin Sanitary Association
FCCA	Fingal County Council Archives
HC	House of Commons
NA	National Archives
NUI	National University of Ireland
NDRDC	North Dublin Rural District Council
NDU	North Dublin Union
OS	Ordnance Survey of Ireland
RCPI	Royal College of Physicians of Ireland
RCSI	Royal College of Surgeons in Ireland
SDRDC	South Dublin Rural District Council
SDU	South Dublin Union
Stat. Soc. Inq. Soc. Ir.	*Statistical and Social Inquiry Society of Ireland*

INTRODUCTION

1 J.T. Gilbert, *History of the city of Dublin*, (3 vols, Dublin, 1854–9); J.T. Gilbert, *Calendar of the ancient records of Dublin* (18 vols, Dublin, 1889–1907).

2 See for example, John D'Alton, *The history of County Dublin* (Dublin, 1838); D.A. Chart, *The story of Dublin* (London, 1907); M.J. Craig, *Dublin, 1660–1860* (Dublin, 1952); F.H.A. Aalen and Kevin Whelan (eds.), *Dublin city and county: from prehistory to present* (Dublin, 1992). Of great value to this particular study however, was a work by Weston St John Joyce entitled *The neighbourhood of Dublin* (Dublin, 1912). Originally intended as a history of Dublin's suburbs, Joyce recorded some very interesting and readable descriptions as he cycled about the county.

3 M.E. Daly, *Dublin the deposed capital: a social and economic history 1860–1914* (Cork, 1985); Jacinta Prunty, *Dublin slums, 1800–1925: a study in urban geography* (Dublin, 1998).

4 This study is based on F.J. Cullen, 'The sanitary campaign in rural Dublin, 1890–1910' MA thesis, Department of Modern History, NUI Maynooth, 1999.

5 F.C.C.A., Minutes of the proceedings of the Board of Guardians of the South Dublin Union acting as the Rural Sanitary Authority under the Public Health Acts, BG 79/A4, 7 November 1898 (hereafter SDU minutes).

6 See for example, Samuel Clarke, *Social origins of the Irish land war* (Princeton, N.J., 1979), and 'Landlord domination in nineteenth-century Ireland', in *Unesco yearbook on peace and conflict studies* (1986), pp. 7–29; J.S. Donnelly, *Landlord and tenant in nineteenth-century Ireland* (Dublin, 1973); W.E. Vaughan, *Landlords and tenants in Ireland, 1848–1904* (Dublin, 1984); K.T. Hoppen, 'Landlords, society and electoral politics in mid-nineteenth-century Ireland', in C.H.E. Philpin (ed.), *Nationalism and popular protest in Ireland* (Cambridge, 1987), pp. 284–319.

GEOGRAPHICAL PERSPECTIVES: THE SOUTH DUBLIN POOR LAW UNION

1 The Public Health (Ireland) Act, 1878, section 6.

2 Peter Collins, *Pathways to Ulster's past: sources and resources for local studies* (Belfast, 1998), p. 5.

3 Virginia Crossman, *Local government in nineteenth-century Ireland* (Belfast, 1994), p. 50.
4 1 & 2 Vict., c. 56 (31 July 1838).
5 William Nolan, *Tracing the past: sources for local studies in the Republic of Ireland* (Dublin, 1982), p. 15.
6 Crossman, *Local government*, p. 46.
7 Crossman, *Local government*, p. 51.
8 Sir George Nicholls, *A history of the Irish Poor Law, in connexion with the condition of the people* (London, 1856), pp. 247, 251.
9 Nicholls, *Irish Poor Law*, pp. 250, 251.
10 *Thom's Directory* (1916).
11 N.A., Minutes of the South Dublin Union workhouse, Dr Steeven's Accession, 10 April 1901 (hereafter SDU minutes Dr Steeven's).
12 N.A., SDU minutes Dr Steeven's, 11 January 1901.
13 *Thom's Directory* (1930).
14 *Thom's Directory* (1890).
15 D'Alton, *County Dublin*.
16 *Thom's Directory* (1890).
17 Weston St John Joyce, *Neighbourhood*.
18 D'Alton, *County Dublin*.
19 Joyce, *Neighbourhood*.

ENVIRONMENTAL MANAGEMENT:
PUBLIC HEALTH CHALLENGES

1 The Public Health (Ireland) Act, 1878, section 11.
2 F.C.C.A., Minutes of the South Dublin Rural District Council, RDC 79/A4, 12 June 1901 (hereafter SDRDC minutes).
3 Jacinta Prunty, *Dublin slums, 1800–1925: a study in urban geography* (Dublin, 1998), p. 159.
4 Joseph Robins, *The miasma: epidemic and panic in nineteenth-century Ireland* (Dublin, 1995), p. 240.
5 *Report of the Executive Committee of the Dublin Sanitary Association, for the year ending May 31, 1878, presented to the sixth annual general meeting, held June 13th, 1878, with rules of the association, list of members, and appendix* (Dublin, 1878), (hereafter *DSA report* 1878).
6 Robins, *Miasma,* p. 240.
7 Robins, *Miasma*, pp. 225–9.
8 F.C.C.A., South Dublin Union minutes BG 79/A4, 7 January 1899 (hereafter SDU minutes).
9 For a detailed analysis of the Public Health (Ireland) Act, 1878, see Francis J. Cullen, 'The sanitary campaign in rural Dublin, 1890–1910', MA thesis, N.U.I. Maynooth, 1999, Chapter Two.
10 F.C.C.A., SDRDC minutes RCD 79/A2, 2 May 1900.
11 F.C.C.A., SDU minutes BG 79/A3, 13 April 1891.
12 F.C.C.A., SDU minutes BG 79/A4, 22 August 1898.
13 F.C.C.A., SDU minutes BG 79/A4, 30 August 1898.
14 F.C.C.A., SDU minutes BG 79/A4, 30 August 1898.
15 The Public Health (Ireland) Act, 1878, section 78.
16 39 & 40 Vict., c.75. This act gave full power to every sanitary authority to institute proceedings against any other sanitary authority or person in respect of offences against said Act, and one of such offences was to cause to fall or flow, or knowingly permit to fall or flow, or to be carried into any stream, any solid or liquid sewage matter; and for the purposes of said Act the expression 'stream' includes rivers, streams, canals, lakes, and watercourses.
17 F.C.C.A., SDU minutes BG 79/A4, 17 October 1898.
18 Weston St John Joyce, *The neighbourhood of Dublin* (1920).
19 F.C.C.A., SDU minutes BG 79/A4, 10 October 1898.
20 See Robins, *Miasma*, pp. 202–32.
21 F.C.C.A., SDU minutes BG 79/A4, 7 January 1899.
22 F.C.C.A., SDU minutes BG 79/A4, 17 October 1898.
23 F.C.C.A., SDU minutes BG 79/A4, 17 October 1898 and BG 79A3, 12 June 1893.
24 Robins, *Miasma*, p. 63.
25 Robins, *Miasma*, pp. 62–110.
26 'Enteric fever is caused by bacterial infection with either Salmonella typhi or Salmonella paratyphi A, B or C. These

infections are called typhoid fever and paratyphoid fever respectively.

Transmission usually occurs by ingestion of water or food that has been contaminated with human faeces, for example, by drinking water contaminated with sewage, or foods prepared by a cook infected with or carrying the organisms'. Gordon Macpherson (ed.), *Black's Medical Dictionary*, (39th ed., London, 1999).

27 F.C.C.A., SDU minutes BG 79/A3.

28 F.C.C.A., SDU minutes BG 79/A3, July, August and September 1891.

29 F.C.C.A., SDU minutes BG 79/A3, 10 August 1891.

30 F.C.C.A., SDU minutes BG 79/A4, 30 August 1898.

31 F.C.C.A., SDU minutes BG 79/A4, 7 November 1898.

32 F.C.C.A., SDU minutes BG 79/A3, 5 October 1891.

33 F.C.C.A., SDU minutes BG 79/A3, 16 February 1891 and 5 October 1891.

34 F.C.C.A., North Dublin Rural District Council minutes RDC 78/A4, 22 June 1904 (hereafter NDRDC minutes).

35 F.C.C.A., SDU minutes BG 79/A3, 29 June 1891.

36 F.C.C.A., SDRDC minutes RDC 79/A2, 4 March 1901.

37 F.C.C.A., SDRDC minutes RDC 79/A2, 4 March 1901.

38 F.C.C.A., NDRDC minutes RDC 78/A4, 2 November 1904.

39 F.C.C.A., SDU minutes BG 79/A4, 20 October 1898.

40 F.C.C.A., SDU minutes BG 79/A4, 6 June 1898.

41 F.C.C.A., SDRDC minutes RDC 79/A3, 3 & 10 October 1900.

42 F.C.C.A., SDRDC minutes RDC 79/A3, 21 November 1900.

43 The Public Health (Ireland) Act, 1878, section 107.

44 F.C.C.A., SDU minutes BG 79/A3, 25 April 1893.

45 F.C.C.A., SDU minutes BG 79/A3, 12 June 1893.

46 F.C.C.A., SDU minutes BG 79/A3, 12 June 1893.

47 F.C.C.A., SDU minutes BG 79/A3, 12 June 1893.

48 F.C.C.A., SDRDC minutes RDC 79/A2, 23 May 1900.

49 F.C.C.A., South Dublin Rural District Council letters to the board, 25 September 1911 (hereafter SDRDC letters).

50 F.C.C.A., SDRDC minutes RDC 79/A3, 17 October 1900.

51 R.C.P.I., Dublin Sanitary Association minutes, 24 July 1884 (hereafter DSA minutes).

52 N.A., Minutes of the South Dublin Union workhouse, Dr Steeven's Accession BG 79 2, 31 May and 7 June 1883 (hereafter SDU minutes Dr Steeven's).

53 DSA report 1878.

54 DSA report 1878, p. 34.

55 DSA report 1878, p. 34.

56 E.D. Mapother, *The unhealthiness of Irish towns, and the want of sanitary legislation*, read before the *Stat. Soc. Inq. Soc. Ir.*, 19 December 1865, (Dublin, 1866).

57 For definition of 'enteric fever' see *Black's Medical Dictionary* quoted above, n. 26.

58 F.C.C.A., SDU minutes BG 79/A3, June, July and August 1891.

59 F.C.C.A., SDU minutes BG 79/A3, June and August 1891, also 27 July 1891.

60 F.C.C.A., SDRDC minutes RDC 79/A2, 3 August 1900.

61 F.C.C.A., SDRDC minutes RDC 79/A3, 21 November 1900.

62 Charles Cameron, *Report upon the state of public health in the city of Dublin for the year 1909* (Dublin, 1910), p. 54.

63 F.C.C.A., SDU minutes BG 79/A4, 18 July 1898.

64 F.C.C.A., SDU minutes BG 79/A4, 22 August 1898.

65 F.C.C.A., SDU minutes BG 79/A4, 10 October 1898.

66 F.C.C.A., SDU minutes BG 79/A3, 7 December 1891.

RURAL HOUSING REFORM: ADDRESSING THE PLIGHT OF THE AGRICULTURAL LABOURER

1 *The Irish Builder*, 8 October 1883.

2 F.H.A. Aalen, 'The rehousing of rural labourers in Ireland under the Labourers' (Ireland) Acts, 1883–1919' in *Journal of historical geography*, xii (1986),

and 'Health and housing in Dublin 1850–1921' in F.H.A. Aalen and K. Whelan (eds.), *Dublin city and county: from prehistory to present* (Dublin, 1992); Murray Fraser, *John Bull's other homes: state housing and British policy in Ireland, 1883–1922* (Liverpool, 1996).

3 Aalen, 'The rehousing of rural labourers', pp. 290–291.

4 R.V. Comerford, in W.E. Vaughan (ed.), *A new history of Ireland VI: Ireland under the union, II 1870–1921* (Oxford, 1996), p. 55.

5 Charles Stewart Parnell speaking in Dublin on 21 August 1882, quotation taken from D.B. King, *The Irish question* (London, 1882), p. 275.

6 King, *The Irish question*, p. 275.

7 Fraser, *John Bull's other homes*, p. 27.

8 *Report of the Vice-Regal Commission on poor law reform in Ireland* Vol. 1, cd 3202 II (1906), reference is made to an 1830s Royal Commission recommending the building of labourers' cottages with small plots attached.

9 King, *The Irish question*, p. 20.

10 *The Irish Builder*, 15 December 1884.

11 *The Irish Builder*, 8 October 1883.

12 F.C.C.A., South Dublin Rural District Council minutes RDC 79/A3, 3 October 1900 (hereafter SDRDC minutes).

13 F.C.C.A., SDRDC minutes RDC 79/A2–4.

14 F.C.C.A., SDRDC minutes RDC 79/A2, 6 June 1900.

15 F.C.C.A., SDRDC minutes RDC 79/A2, 27 February 1901.

16 F.C.C.A., South Dublin Union minutes BG 79/A4, 17 October 1898 (hereafter SDU minutes).

17 F.C.C.A., SDU minutes BG 79/A4, 17 October 1898.

18 F.C.C.A., SDU minutes BG 79/A4, 7 January 1899.

19 F.C.C.A., SDU minutes BG 79/A4, 24 October 1898.

20 F.C.C.A., SDRDC minutes RDC 79/A6, 27 August and 10 September 1902.

21 F.C.C.A., SDU minutes BG 79/A4, 6 June 1898.

22 F.C.C.A., SDRDC minutes RDC 79/A2, 1 August 1900.

23 F.C.C.A., SDRDC minutes RDC 79/A2, 22 August 1900.

24 F.C.C.A., SDRDC minutes RDC 79/A2, 26 December 1900.

25 In 1944 two possible origins of the placename Bushelloaf were given: 'It is not improbable that the Bushelloaf was an inn the name of which according to fading tradition became that of the townland' [or] 'Quite a different origin for the name was heard fully sixty years ago from an old man who held a good share of folklore. In penal times according to him a priest captured here was kept tied to a bush until he died of hunger whilst before his eyes, but beyond his reach, a loaf remained suspended from the same bush; hence the place was afterwards called Bush and Loaf and now Bush a' Loaf'., in Liam Ua Broin, 'Clondalkin, Co. Dublin, and its neighbourhood: notes on placenames, topography and traditions, &c', in *Journal of the Royal Society of Antiquaries of Ireland*, lxxiv, (1944), pp. 191–218.

26 F.C.C.A., SDRDC minutes RDC 79/A2, 12, 26 September and 3 October 1900.

27 F.C.C.A., SDRDC minutes RDC 79/A3, 20 November 1900.

28 F.C.C.A., SDRDC minutes RDC 79/A4, 1 May 1901.

29 F.C.C.A., SDRDC minutes RDC 79/A4, 24 July 1901.

30 F.C.C.A., SDRDC minutes RDC 79/A4, 11 September 1901.

31 F.C.C.A., SDRDC minutes RDC 79/A3, 6 January 1901.

32 See F.C.C.A., SDRDC minutes RDC 79/A4, July 1901 and South Dublin Rural District Council letters to the board, 1911 (hereafter SDRDC letters).

33 See n. 19 in second chapter 'Geographical perspectives: the South Dublin Poor Law Union'.

34 F.C.C.A., SDRDC minutes RDC 79/A4, 16 November 1900.

35 F.C.C.A., SDRDC minutes RDC 79/A4, 16 January 1901.

36 F.C.C.A., SDRDC minutes RDC 79/A3, 20 February 1901.

37 See Francis J. Cullen, 'The sanitary campaign in rural Dublin, 1890–1910'

MA thesis, NUI Maynooth, 1999, pp 48–53.

38 F.C.C.A., SDRDC minutes RDC 79/A4, 1 May 1901.

39 Extract of letter by J.C. Madden to South Dublin Rural District Council, in F.C.C.A., SDRDC minutes RDC 79/A4, 18 September 1901.

40 F.C.C.A., SDRDC minutes RDC 79/A4, 31 July 1901.

41 *Thom's Dublin Street Directory* (1998).

42 F.C.C.A., SDU minutes BG 79/A2, 22 December 1890.

43 F.C.C.A., SDU minutes BG 79/A2, 22 December 1890.

44 F.C.C.A., SDRDC letters, 4 October 1911.

45 F.C.C.A., SDRDC letters, 24 October 1911.

46 F.C.C.A., SDRDC letters, 29 November 1911.

47 F.C.C.A., SDRDC letters, 29 November 1911.

48 F.C.C.A., SDRDC letters, 14 November 1911.

49 Nicholas J. Synnott, *The housing of the rural population in Ireland: a review of the Labourers' Acts*, A paper read before the *Statistical and Social Inquiry Society of Ireland*, 27 November 1903 (Dublin, 1904) pp. 7–8 (hereafter Synnott, *Housing*).

50 Synnott, *Housing*, pp. 7–8.

51 *Annual report of the local government board for Ireland for the year ended 31 Mar. 1920*, p. lxxvi [Cmd 1423], H.C. 1921, xiv, 858., in W.E. Vaughan (ed.), *A new history of Ireland VI: Ireland under the union, II 1870–1921* (Oxford, 1996), p. 277.

52 See Aalen, 'The rehousing of rural labourers', and Fraser, *John Bull's other homes.*

53 Synnott, *Housing*, and *Proposals for a new Labourers' Bill: an attempt to solve the rural housing question in Ireland* (Naas, 1906).

54 Synnott, *Housing*, preface.

Maynooth Research Guides for Irish Local History

IN THIS SERIES

1 Raymond Refaussé, *Church of Ireland Records*
2 Terry Dooley, *Sources for the History of Landed estates in Ireland*
3 Patrick J. Corish and David Sheehy, *Records of the Irish Catholic Church*
4 Jacinta Prunty, *Maps and Mapmaking in Local History*

Maynooth Studies in Irish Local History

IN THIS SERIES

1 Paul Connell, *Parson, Priest and Master: National Education in Co. Meath 1824–41*

2 Denis A. Cronin, *A Galway Gentleman in the Age of Improvement: Robert French of Monivea, 1716–79*

3 Brian Ó Dálaigh, *Ennis in the 18th Century: Portrait of an Urban Community*

4 Séamas Ó Maitiú, *The Humours of Donnybrook: Dublin's Famous Fair and its Suppression*

5 David Broderick, *An Early Toll-Road: The Dublin–Dunleer Turnpike, 1731–1855*

6 John Crawford, *St Catherine's Parish, Dublin 1840–1900: Portrait of a Church of Ireland Community*

7 William Gacquin, *Roscommon Before the Famine: The Parishes of Kiltoom and Cam, 1749–1845*

8 Francis Kelly, *Window on a Catholic Parish: St Mary's Granard, Co. Longford, 1933–68*

9 Charles V. Smith, *Dalkey: Society and Economy in a Small Medieval Irish Town*

10 Desmond J. O'Dowd, *Changing Times: Religion and Society in Nineteenth-Century Celbridge*

11 Proinnsíos Ó Duigneáin, *The Priest and the Protestant Woman*

12 Thomas King, *Carlow: the manor and town, 1674–1721*

13 Joseph Byrne, *War and Peace: The Survival of the Talbots of Malahide 1641–1671*

14 Bob Cullen, *Thomas L. Synnott: The Career of a Dublin Catholic 1830–70*

15 Helen Sheil, *Falling into Wretchedness: Ferbane in the late 1830s*

16 Jim Gilligan, *Graziers and Grasslands: Portrait of a Rural Meath Community 1854–1914*

17 Miriam Lambe, *A Tipperary Estate: Castle Otway, Templederry 1750–1853*

18 Liam Clare, *Victorian Bray: A Town Adapts to Changing Times*

Maynooth Studies in Irish Local History (cont.)

19 Ned McHugh, *Drogheda before the Famine: Urban Poverty in the Shadow of Privilege 1826–45*

20 Toby Barnard, *The Abduction of a Limerick Heiress: Social and political relations in mid eighteenth-century Ireland*

21 Seamus O'Brien, *Famine and Community in Mullingar Poor Law Union, 1845–1849: Mud Huts and Fat Bullocks*

22 Séamus Fitzgerald, *Mackerel and the Making of Baltimore, Co. Cork, 1879–1913*

23 Íde Ní Liatháin, *The Life and Career of P.A. McHugh, 1859–1909: A Footsoldier of the Party*

24 Miriam Moffitt, *The Church of Ireland Community of Killala and Achonry 1870–1940*

25 Ann Murtagh, *Portrait of a Westmeath Tenant Community, 1879–85: The Barbavilla Murder*

26 Jim Lenehan, *Politics and Society in Athlone, 1830–1885: A Rotten Borough*

27 Anne Coleman, *Riotous Roscommon: Social Unrest in the 1840s*

28 Maighréad Ní Mhurchadha, *The Customs and Excise service in Fingal, 1684–1765: Sober, Active and Bred to the Sea*

29 Chris Lawlor, *Canon Frederick Donovan's Dunlavin 1884–1896: A west Wicklow village in the late nineteenth century*

30 Eithne Massey, *Prior Roger Outlaw of Kilmainham*

31 Terence A.M. Dooley, *The Plight of the Monaghan Protestants, 1912–26*

32 Patricia Friel, *Frederick Trench, 1746–1836 and Heywood, Queen's County the creation of a romantic landscape*

33 Tom Hunt, *Portlaw, county Waterford 1825–76, Portrait of an industrial village and its cotton industry.*

34 Brian Gurrin, *A century of struggle in Delgany and Kilcoole: An exploration of the social implications of population change in north-east Wicklow, 1666–1779*

35 William H. Crawford, *The Management of a Major Ulster Estate in the Late Eighteenth Century. The Eighth Earl of Abercorn and his Irish Agents*

36 Maeve Mulryan Moloney, *Nineteenth-century elementary education in the archdiocese of Tuam*

37 Fintan Lane, *In Search of Thomas Sheahan: Radical Politics in Cork, 1824–1836*

38 Anthony Doyle, *Charles Powell Leslie (II)'s estates at Glaslough, County Monaghan, 1800–41: Portrait of a landed estate business and its community in changing times*

39 Mealla C. Ní Ghiobúin, *Dugort, Achill Island, 1831–1861: A study of the rise and fall of a missionary community*

40 Frank Cullen, *Cleansing rural Dublin: public health and housing initiatives in the South Dublin poor law union 1880–1920*